BE THE CHANGE

BE THE CHANGE

Poems, Prayers and Meditations for
Peacemakers and Justice Seekers

Stephen Shick

SKINNER HOUSE BOOKS
BOSTON

Printed in the United States

Cover and text design by Suzanne Morgan
Cover art © 2005 Christine Destrempes, www.destrempes.com

print ISBN: 978-1-55896-549-2
eBook ISBN: 978-1-55896-593-5

6 5 4
20 19 18 17
Some of the selections are formatted in a call-and-response style.
These responsive readings are well-suited for use in worship.

Library of Congress Cataloging-in-Publication Data

Shick, Stephen M.
  Be the change : poems, prayers, and meditations for peacemakers
and justice seekers / Stephen Shick.
     p. cm.
  ISBN-13: 978-1-55896-549-2 (pbk. : alk. paper)
  ISBN-10: 1-55896-549-1 (pbk. : alk. paper) 1. Spiritual life—
Unitarian Universalist Association. 2. Unitarian Universalist Associa-
tion—Prayers and devotions. 3. Peace—Religious aspects—Unitarian
Universalist Association. 4. Christianity and justice. I. Title.
  BX9855.S54 2009
  261.8'73—dc22
                                                        2008040685

We gratefully acknowledge permission to reprint the following:
excerpt from "One Song" by Jalal Al-Din Rumi, translated by Coleman
Barks, from The Soul of Rumi: A New Collection of Ecstatic Poems,
reprinted by permission of Coleman Barks; excerpt from "Beginners"
by Denise Levertov, from Candles in Babylon, copyright © 1982 by
Denise Levertov, reprinted by permission of New Directions Publishing
Corp.

For JoAnn,
whose love continues
to open my life
to new possibilities

CONTENTS

Being a Force of Nature

FOREWORD

During my twelve years as Executive Director of Amnesty International USA, I learned a great deal about the dynamics of rescue. Almost all work for social justice involves some type of rescue—be it rescue of individual sufferers, as was often the case at Amnesty, or rescue of a society at large, or even rescue of our ideals from the lurch of despond. In this book Stephen Shick, a lifelong activist whom I have known and respected since he headed up the Unitarian Universalist Peace Network over twenty years ago, provides an invaluable guide to the navigation of rescue.

Many times of course we fail to achieve a rescue and the result can be bitterness or retreat. But, in a funny kind of way, being successful can also be fraught with difficulties.

The dynamic between the rescuer and the rescued is tricky. On the one hand, the person who is rescued is enormously grateful for the relief of her torment—be that homelessness, poverty, unjust imprisonment, torture—and often expresses that gratitude liberally to whomever she believes responsible for the relief. Such a reaction is entirely natural, but it reflects a power differential between rescuer and rescued that can shade into resentment later. No one likes to feel that her fate has been determined by somebody else. The expression often heard from the person who is rescued, "I can't thank you *enough*," is very telling. "You have saved my life (or my home or my children's future) and I will *always* be indebted to you." That is, I feel as if I can never pay you back sufficiently and therefore you will always have some kind of claim on me.

From the point of view of the rescuer, the danger in a successful rescue is not resentment but pride. "Look what we have accomplished—we have fought the dragon and we have won. We have saved the Kingdom from the forces of evil." Pride entices us not only to think we know all the answers but to be supremely irritated with all the others who think that they do too!

This kind of righteous anger is quite common among people who work for a more just society. And it makes sense that we would be angry at unjust conditions in society such as greed, racism, and violence. These feelings can be motivating.

But I am talking about another kind of anger that appears too often: an anger so pervasive that it targets not only oppressors but allies who see the problem differently; that prevents us from seeing the humanity in our opponents; that mistakes righteousness for being right. I will never forget one Sunday morning listening to a preacher, his face red with rage, pounding the pulpit as he commanded his parishioners "to be *gentle* with each other!"

And along with anger comes guilt—guilt that we cannot do more, that we are implicated by this filthy society we are trying to repair. At Amnesty International our work really could be a matter of someone else's life or death. In the face of that responsibility, how could we ever rest? I spent a great deal of time reminding activists and volunteers that an exhausted person was an ineffective agent for change; that staying healthy, energized, and inspired was itself a gift to the victims; and that a world not worth experiencing in all its glory and wonder was not a world worth saving. A medical doctor who had been imprisoned in a Nazi concentration camp and had done much good for his fellow prisoners once was asked how he had managed to survive. He replied, "My rule was very simple: It was myself first and then myself again and then myself a third time and then all the others."

So these are some of the pitfalls of being a rescuer: pride, anger, guilt. They require for their repair a sense of balance and larger purpose, a quiet at the center, a deep appreciation of the gracious and the grand—all of which this remarkable book provides. And one thing more.

Often, as I said at the outset, despite our best efforts we fail to win a newer world. At times like that we look for reminders that, with all its flaws, Creation contains enormous gifts and, despite our limitations, when we live with tenderness and care, our very presence can be a manifestation of Creation's grace. We are reminded of that too within the pages of this book.

"How can you hear day after day about terrible atrocities like torture and genocide and still manage to go on?" I would often be asked during my years with Amnesty. And I would reply by saying that, difficult as it was to hear about such things, it was far worse to experience them. I would say that it had been my privilege to meet dozens of people who had been tortured or had loved ones murdered but who with help had managed, despite all that suffering, to emerge from their experiences with a deep commitment to humanity, determined not to allow the perpetrators to crush their spirits even as they had abused their bodies. The least I could do was hear their stories and help give voice to their determination. And then I might add that though at the end of a long day I often lost my faith in our ability to make a difference or in the possibility of a better world, I was grateful to have re-gained that faith with the arrival of a new day.

All that I said in reply to my questioners was true. But the really important question was not how *I* survived the stories but how the targets of human rights crimes survived their ordeals. And the answer that I received from one after another when I asked them was that they fastened onto something—their family; their comrades; their ideals; the cause in which they believed—and held on, certain in the faith that eventually their suffering would end.

Sometimes it did and sometimes it didn't. But either way, the imperative at hand was to *hold on*. And, be we rescuer or rescued, that is always the imperative for those who seek to tame the forces of injustice: to hold on, to sustain the vision, to keep the faith. In Stephen Shick we find an inspiring guide to show us how.

—William F. Schulz

Currently a senior fellow in human rights policy at the Center for American Progress, William F. Schulz served as president of the Unitarian Universalist Association from 1985 to 1993 and executive director of Amnesty International USA from 1994 to 2006.

INTRODUCTION

In 1969, during the war in Vietnam, I applied for a job in the peace movement and received in response a handwritten letter from Sandy Gottlieb, the director of the Committee for a Sane Nuclear Policy. He didn't have a job for me, but he offered this observation: "What the peace movement needs are long-distance runners." At the time this insight seemed irrelevant to ending the war and creating a more just society in America.

Now, four decades later, I realize what I didn't understand back then. Being a long-distance runner in the quest for peace and justice is an art. We don't need a fancy title or a special position. Instead, we need to understand ourselves, to have some perspective on our work and our place in life. And we need to keep ourselves open to moments of grace and inspiration when they come our way.

Today's world is plagued with problems. We are caught up in cycles of war, injustice, and revenge while millions are trapped in poverty. The depths of the problems can overwhelm even the most passionate among us or turn the most compassionate into cynics. Although this has happened to me at times too, I have chosen to continue to work for justice on a variety of national and local issues. These efforts have included educating and protesting to end the Vietnam War and the nuclear arms race, helping improve the lives of children living in poverty through lobbying and organizing, and working locally on behalf of the homeless and hungry. When I began all this, I didn't know how long I'd last, but with a lot of good luck and a little wisdom picked up along the way, I've made it this far and plan to keep going.

Every human being naturally possesses the power to initiate and sustain positive change. Howard Thurman, considered by many the spiritual guide of the civil rights movement, wrote that in each person there is a calm sea where she can discover her own infinite self-worth. Discovering this allows us to more effectively and lovingly speak truth to power. The poems, meditations, prayers, and litanies in this collection flow from this belief.

Perhaps you are considering for the first time what you might do to address one or more of the problems facing humankind. Perhaps you have been doing this kind of work for decades. In either case, I hope this book helps to sustain you on your journey. I wish I had read a book like this when I began or had it with me during those times when I was paralyzed by my own weaknesses and lack of resilience.

For periods of time I have lost all perspective. To regain perspective is itself a spiritual practice, one that involves our awareness of the vast scope of nature and the far reaches of human history. From this wider view we realize that change is inevitable. Despite our small failures, we can bend the universe toward justice while celebrating life as an incredible gift that unfolds in rhythms and cycles beyond human control.

It is humbling to realize that all of us stand on the front lines of history, with innumerable human mistakes and achievements behind us, and that we are part of an endless cycle of nature's evolutionary successes and failures. Nature and history reveal a fundamental paradox: Everything we believe and everything we do are both very insignificant and ultimately crucial. Learning to live with this paradox helps us discover our power to change the world for the better, but we can't do the work effectively without knowing when to rest from it.

Spiritual or mindfulness practice can increase our awareness of the unexpected gifts that fill life with beauty and insight. Jelaluddin Rumi, the thirteenth-century Sufi mystic, reminds us that even tragedy can be "a gift from beyond," one that frees us for new delights. The mystery and power of the universe, while beyond our understanding, continue to arrive in ways that can renew our spirits and awaken us to what is possible.

Reflecting this process toward mindfulness, the first chapter, "Reflecting Inward," explores the need for inner calm in order to nurture hope and to do this difficult work. "Being a Force of Nature" and "Being a Force of History" are about owning one's power and gaining perspective. These are hard things to achieve and maintain when the cause is just and the stakes are high. "Practice" addresses the spiritual practices and self-care that help us maintain our balance, and the final chapter, "Arriving Grace" honors the mystical realm that eludes rational understanding and yet continues to surprise and sustain us in our darkest moments.

In a radio series I produced long ago, Studs Terkel, the intrepid Chicago radio personality and author, said something like this: "I wake up in the morning and read the papers and say the human species is not going to make it. Then," he continued, "I run into people who are making a difference. . . ." I offer this book to those people, to you, who look upon the carnage of war, the cruelty of poverty, and the destruction of our environment with open eyes and simply say, "We can and must do better." This book is for you who, despite fears and limitations, give hope and courage to all of us by the way you live. It is dedicated to you who have a pestering need to love more boldly and live more courageously so that others might live better lives.

—Stephen M. Shick
January 2009

REFLECTING INWARD

Jesus said, "One who knows all but is lacking in oneself is utterly lacking."

—Gospel of Thomas

THE GIFT OF SABBATH

Spirit of my greatest longing, help me accept the gift of Sabbath—a moment, an hour, a day of awareness that will return to me again and again. Like the unnamed one who quieted the waters of chaos to bring all things to life, grant me the wisdom of the pause. Help me still the churning waters of my soul.

A POLISHED MIRROR

Polish your heart for a day or two; make that mirror your book of contemplation.

—Rumi

Honestly searching our hearts, we find our true self, the one that is strong enough to confess errors, open-minded enough to change direction, and wise enough to live generously so others might simply live. When we polish the interior mirror of the self, it shines upon our longings for peace and justice and gives off the radiance of insight.

For years my life was filled with working to end militarism and establish new government priorities. There were local and national demonstrations to plan, speeches to give, and broadcasts to make. Self-reflection seemed a wasteful indulgence. Then suddenly my personal life began to unravel, and I was forced to begin an inward journey that eventually cast a sustaining light on my work for peace and justice.

The need for contemplation is never-ending. The true self lurks in the shadows of ever-changing circumstances. With the polished mirror of self-reflection, however, we are able to see more clearly those qualities of self that diminish our potential and are able to be more at peace in any situation.

Loving in Fear

Spirit of Life, God of Love, grant me the courage to love boldly in the face of my greatest fears. Grow me in your wisdom and let my actions speak when silence threatens justice and indifference disturbs peace. When gossip, hate, and cruelty arise among friends or in public places, help me bravely walk forward with love. When I defensively assert certainty in the presence of the unknown, grant me the courage to live comfortably in the unanswerable questions of life. Bless me with the eternal gift of not knowing and let it take root in me until it pushes forth shoots of understanding and branches of humility.

Living Waters

We float on a sea
hidden beneath dry surfaces
covered by stones.

Isn't this why we drink and dive so deeply
go down to the sea in ships
risk drowning, again and again?

Isn't this why Moses parted the waters
to begin his journey?

Why Jesus crossed the waters
to comfort and challenge us?

We were born in water.
We float free in water.
We are washed clean by water.

Isn't this why we long to find our inward sea?
To help us wash clean the world?

When Nothing Is the Same

For no two successive days is the shoreline precisely the same. Not only do the tides advance and retreat in their eternal rhythms, but the level of the sea itself is never at rest.

—Rachel Carson

Deep within the earth, heat from a boiling sea of iron sets forces in motion that elevate mountains, change the level of the oceans, and flip magnetic poles. Yet, in the midst of all this, there is uniformity and consistency. The sun rises and sets. The seasons change. Living things are born and die in an endless cycle.

Like the earth, we thrive on change and depend on stability. Each day our reactions to the shifting contours of our lives are different. Each day the depth of our resilience changes. Knowing this, we flourish like life on a changing shoreline.

Self-Honesty

The nation was wealthy and militarily powerful. Some people had grown rich at the expense of many who lived in poverty. Leaders became conceited, certain their prosperity and security were only due to their own efforts.

Amos, a Hebrew prophet from a poor rural region, grasped the moral significance of the growing gap between the rich and poor and of the nation's arrogance. He saw Israel headed for self-destruction unless it woke up and reflected honestly about itself. So he fashioned a speech whose simple truth speaks to us today. He knew his people would close their ears if he began by telling them what was wrong with their behavior, so he drew them in with a rhetorical trick which played to their self-righteousness. He said that the nations surrounding Israel would suffer God's wrath for neglecting the poor and for their egotism. He named all their wrongdoings. Then this humble prophet turned his attention to Israel and lay open its failings, showing how they would lead to ruin.

Amos got the attention of his people by asking them to do what we all do so naturally—focus on the negative behavior of our enemies while ignoring our own weaknesses. Another prophet of Israel, Jesus of Nazareth, found a simple way to say it: "Why do you notice the sliver in your friend's eye, but overlook the timber in your own?"

In the midst of injustice and arrogance, let us speak skillfully and humbly, and pray for the wisdom to examine our own hearts.

Revealing Rings

The cutting was complete.
The aged contours of the tree lay at his feet.
All the young scientist wanted was there now
in the secrets of the rings
    the glory of discovery
    the victory of new knowledge
    the pride of accomplishment.

He counted past the ring of Jesus' birth,
Buddha's enlightenment,
the writing of the most sacred Vedic texts.

Then he moved beyond the year 4800
and discovered
he had destroyed
the oldest living thing,
severing its connection to the ground of being
    the only true source of knowledge
    the only true source of glory.

Take Off Your Mask

*Love takes off the mask we fear we cannot live without and know
we cannot live within.*

—James Baldwin

We reach for the mask of righteousness
when our insecurities are exposed,
slip it over purple scars
and yellowing bruises we gained
when, open-faced,
we first met our fears.

Once inside our mask
comfort fills our lungs
and our breathing softens.

No one told us the dangers of living behind the mask,
of what happens when tears fall in darkness
and do not wash away arrogance and pride.

No one told us how life fades
from faces untouched by opposition.
But now that we know,
will you help me lift my mask?
And if you'll let me, I'll help to lift yours.

Mother Renewal

Spirit of Life, mother of all my impulses to love, give me courage to leave the comfort of my birth place and discover your sustaining power wherever I go. Let me gratefully embrace this day and each moment as it opens into newness. When I grow impatient with living in my own darkness, push me out again into the unfolding uncertainty and wonder of the day. In the moment of my rebirth, I pray that I might grow to become ripe fruit on your tree of life. In the dawn of this new day, may the power of the universe flow through me as it did through you at its beginning, when the dream of love was planted in the human heart.

Dimensions of Soul

And he whose soul is flat—the sky
Will cave in on him by and by.

—Edna St. Vincent Millay

Buckminster Fuller's geodesic dome became the symbol of the World Exposition in 1967 and later the architectural emblem of the Disney Epcot Center. This bold and innovative architectural design flowed from Fuller's multi-dimensional passions. He devoted himself to discovering how modern technology could free human potential. Economical to build and durable in almost any climate, the geodesic dome was intended to solve the global housing shortage. For this work he received the acclaim of the world's leading architects and scientists.

At age thirty-two Buckminster Fuller could not have dreamed of contributing to the betterment of humankind. His soul was flat and in his own eyes he was a failure. A series of personal tragedies had collapsed upon him and he considered suicide.

This all changed when he began a two-year journey into solitude. He said that the goal of his inward travel was to "discover the principles governing the universe" in order to "help advance the evolution of humanity." He explored the depth of his own purpose in life and the height of service to others. As these dimensions grew, he emerged from his self-doubt and depression. He abandoned his ambitions for personal gain and fame and began to see his life as an experiment designed to benefit all people. He called himself "Guinea Pig B." This simple proclamation of living in service to humankind brought purpose to his life. The sky never again caved in on him.

What Are You Doing Here?

Elijah had defeated the forces of King Ahab and Queen Jezebel, proving to his own followers the power of his god. Yet violence followed violence and Elijah was soon set running for his life.

After a day of running he wished for death. Then an angel touched him and urged him on, providing him with food and drink. Forty days later, he arrived at a cave on the holy mountain, where he heard a voice ask, *What are you doing here, Elijah?* He responded self-righteously, saying he alone had been faithful. The voice was not satisfied and commanded him to go to the front of the cave, where the Eternal would pass by. Before he could respond, a great wind ripped apart the mountain, but the Eternal was not revealed in the storm. Then a great earthquake shook the foundations of the earth, but the Eternal was not revealed in the earthquake. Then there came in succession a great fire and sheer silence. But, the Eternal was not in any of these. Then he heard a whisper from within, *What are you doing here, Elijah?* When Elijah finally listened to that inner voice, he heard the words, *Go back the way you came.*

Go back the way you came and face those enemies that set you running for your life. A strange command indeed. If you do this, the voice assured him, you will discover new allies and renewed strength and you will meet Elisha, the one who will inherit your powers of prophecy. Elijah was not being asked to retreat into the past where no one can live. Rather, the voice was asking him to have faith to face the fears he carried inside himself.

If we listen to the inner voice and face our fears, we can discover what needs to be done, here and now.

Grow Restless

To insist that I must be only what I am now is a restriction which human nature must abhor.

—Abraham Heschel

How easy it is to be confident when our cause is just and our opponents make outrageous claims. Who can blame us for a little posturing now and then, for some exaggerating to make a point? However, we must not be confined to the certainty of what is, or blinded to what might be. What could we see if we looked inside ourselves for ways to change and grow, rather than looking outward for the ways others fall short?

To grow restless with who we are helps us move toward our ideals. Perfection is impossible, but we all have the potential to be more patient, more compassionate, more open-minded. When we approach the unattainable self, knowing that our lives are only approximations of what we seek, we free our souls.

When to Take Off Your Sandals

Spirit of my exploring heart, help me walk where deep-rooted questions rise through the firm hard ground, the pathway that has led to war and injustice for centuries. Bare-footed and trembling, let me feel the pain that inhumanity has tramped into the earth. Let me face the unknown, assured that all my questions are natural and blameless. Help me learn how to live peacefully when war and anger rage, how to do justice while greed consumes resources that could sustain us. Bruised and battered, let my feet feel holiness rise through the ground of my being. Let that holiness fill me with confidence, that I might find alternatives to the well-trod roads to destruction. Grant me the wisdom to do as Moses did on that sacred mountain, when he was told "Take off your sandals, for the place where you are standing is holy ground."

THE ETERNAL

It is not old,

> *Yet it comes through the wisdom of the ages.*

It is not young,

> *Yet it comes through the passion of innocence.*

It is not revolutionary,

> *Yet it comes proclaiming change.*

It is not solitary,

> *Yet it travels alone, seeking the open heart.*

It is not lonely,

> *Yet it seeks relationship.*

It is not attached,

> *Yet it connects everything.*

It is the fresh return of the eternal,

> *And it demands our response.*

FREEDOM WAITS

Spirit of Life, God of Love, the image of the freedom train speaks to me today. I have waited so long for a train to arrive and carry me to the promised land of peace and justice. Now, on the platform of indifference and self doubt, I see that the train is here and waiting for me to step on board. Yet someone, a shadow of who I can be, is holding me back saying, *Who are you to ride with those who risked so much for freedom? Who are you to proclaim the sacred message of the inherent worth and dignity of every person?* Now the conductor is calling me to get on board and I must decide what to do. Will I step up and over my own fears and prejudices? Will I dare to ride with the outcast immigrant, the unwashed homeless, the mentally and physically challenged, the hated Jew, Muslim, Christian, Hindu, and Buddhist? Will I speak with compassion and love to all those who disagree with me, who abuse me, who threaten me? Will I risk my comfort to comfort others?

Spirit of my great longing, awaken in me the courage to get on board.

THE LOST DIMENSION

Is a dimension lost?
Is it love?
—Maya Angelou

I awoke to an empty "to-do" list. I vowed that on this day I would put nothing on it. Just let things happen naturally.

I have models for this radical behavior. Every bee, turtle, and muskrat knows to the bone what to do. Puppies know how to find the nipples; their mothers know how long to put up with all that shoving and sucking. The whole world is filled with knowledge of how to live, where to eat, and how much pushing any individual can take.

Why do we hunger for knowledge of what to do? Why do we wrestle, like Jacob and Jesus, with devils and gods to find out how to do it? Is there a gene of ignorance planted deep within us? Were we created a little lower than the angels or just below the puppies? Animals live successfully without being told anything. They love without envy; kill without hatred; sing, chirp, and warble without vanity. They seem to know instinctively how to love life. And what about us— have we lost this dimension? Perhaps.

DREAMS AND FEARS

Our dreams and fears
become entwined
in stories woven over time
and shape the truth
in trembling minds
that want to know
beyond all doubt
what life is all about.

CREATING FIRE

Is the fire going out?
Not in your belly,
for you are still alive,
but in your soul,
that place

> where dreams
> fuel commitment

> where longings
> shape action

> where meaning
> flames purpose

> where passion ignites
> and rekindles
> your life fire.

If your soul smolders
dream on
till you flame
like a chalice of hope.

THEY KNEW

Then Jesus said, "Father, forgive them; for they do not know what they are doing."

—Luke 23:34

I believe Jesus about a lot of things—love your neighbor as yourself, turn the other cheek, cross the street to help someone your friends despise. But I don't believe him when he said that those who crucified him didn't know what they were doing.

They knew, just as I know not to look in the eyes of a beggar, lest I see myself. They knew, just as I know how to get even. They knew, just as I know that the cost of speaking up for the outcast is high.

I have lived a different truth and some day I hope someone will forgive me. Or, I will learn to forgive myself by doing better next time—as he did.

ANCIENT WATERS

Spirit of living earth, God of my loving heart, I sense that deep inside me is enough water to refresh me forever. Hidden in the hot chamber just above the core of my being and concealed in my bone, muscle, and mind, it awaits release. Though invisible from the surface, I have felt these waters lift me, like a wave carrying me back to shore.

Like earth, we rest on water, move in water, and are held together by water. Living on the surface, it is hard to imagine the presence of this renewing reservoir. Cross currents pull me this way and that. They soothe me and invite me to play. They touch me with joy and wash me clean. They roar, crash, crush, and drown everything and everyone in their way. Their currents of debris and torrents of unrelenting rage frighten me.

Spirit of my ever-flowing life, teach me to dive where the ancient waters rest inside me so I might float, forever to be washed with newness and hope.

Useful Anger

A good anger swallowed
clots the blood
to slime
>   —Marge Piercy

But what is to be done with it,
this anger that dare not be swallowed?

Should it be diluted with denial, cooled with indifference?
Should it be sweetened with good intentions,
softened with lies?
Should it be spewed out red hot over searing tongues,
scorching the guilty and innocent alike?

What's to be done with it,
this anger that dare not be swallowed?

Don't dilute it, deny it, or cool it.
Don't sweeten it or soften it.
But, pause for a moment.

Could you hold it before your eyes
    examine it with your heart and mind?
Could you hold it
    then touch it to your belly
    that place where your soul rests?
Could you let it enter there knowing it is the part of you
    that needs to be treated kindly
    that needs to be listened to
    that needs to be honored?

For it has the power to save you,
to save us all.

LIKE A RIVER

God of the flowing river of life, when my heart is light, like the mayfly dancing above your surface, let me rejoice. As I rise and dip through the air currents of my days your presence gives me courage to fly free. And when the rains of sorrow force me to rest on your banks, help me to accept your soothing ripples, promising that despite its pain, life is good. In the darkest, coldest time, as I lie hardened and nearly frozen, let me hear your undercurrents coursing through my veins, awakening my muscles, renewing my mind, seeping purpose into every part of me. In my discerning moments, grant me wisdom to trust what I discover in your endless current of possibilities. Then let me hear the wisdom that flowed through your Sufi poet Rumi:

> *When you do things from your soul, you feel a river moving in you, a joy.*
>
> *When action comes from another section, the feeling disappears.*

Grant me the courage to give back to life all that its flowing river provides.

NEW YEAR GUESTS

Blessed guide to understanding, let me pause at the turning of the new year, as people of the earth have done in different ways for thousands of years. Here on the edge of newness, where hope is sharp and failure not far back on the bevel, help me to break through my numbness and indifference to accept every circumstance as a gracious host and lively companion. If sorrows knock, help me let them in and embrace them until they fall asleep in my arms like a baby. If joy and gladness arrive let me dance with them until the next guest arrives. In this way each day will be new and I will experience joy and sorrow as honored guests in my unfolding life.

OPEN CHAMBERS

Spirit of the loving heart, open the chambers of my deepest
longing. Let your love flow freely through me, awakening
my passions and healing my wounds. Grant me the will to
wade gracefully into your current, letting it lift me above all
the sunken wreckage of my life. Fill me with the courage to
speak lovingly to those who build dams of resentment and
hatred. Fill me with compassion that I might flood over the
embankments that separate me from those wounded in body
or spirit. Let me dissolve my desires and ambitions into the
undercurrent of your renewing and sustaining love.

A SPACE BETWEEN

Now is never
captured in words
or shot still in pictures.

Now is never visited
in museums
or in memories.

Now is never dreamed of
or longed for.

Now is a timeless awareness,
a space between what
has been and what will be,
a lens in the beam of our being
where light can become peace.

My Obit

What if the editor of my obit
    omits that part of my story
    when I found love, or lost it,
    that part when I chose
    not fame or fortune but the passion
    that awakened me to the rest of my life?

What if they forget to tell the preacher
    about the time you forgave me
    and I could breathe again
    as if I had never breathed before?

And what if no one listens
    as the preacher, without emphasis,
    tells of the moment when
    I reached the high notes of my life?

What if, after all I have said and done,
    they forget my favorite stories
    and the way I told them to my children
    again and again?

What if I live so long that even my times
    are forgotten
    and the way we fought non-violently
    for justice and peace?

But wait, what if my story is not a story at all
    but a drop, singing to the river of life?

My Child

Spirit of Light, in the darkest season of our souls we strike
ourselves against life's hard surfaces to release your eternal
newness. We rejoice in the birth of a child of hope. This
child is as old as time and as new as the moment we lift our

match of resolve. On winter's dawn the babe is born, rising in our hearts, spreading warmth on our coldest fears. A gift of time claimed from the chaos of timeless ages. A mystery dissolved into human form? Is he the living Jesus? Is she Shiva, creator of all worlds? This child cares not what we call it, only that we nurture it and let it grow into the dark places where hate grows and despair lingers. This child of love is born each moment we choose what might yet be. Let us rejoice in its holy birth.

THE TREE MIRROR

You have to let your eyes fall more than half-way down its barren trunk before you can see bark. From there to the ground a torn garment covers its naked form. It was dead the first time I saw it. That was over a decade ago. I was delighted how in death it could attract so much life. I have watched hairy and downy woodpeckers, even once a pair of pileated ones, come to feed on its abundant remains.

I have studied this tree, not as a naturalist might, but as an observer of my own soul. It has been a splendid mirror, reflecting back the images I have needed most to see. One summer, while looking at its rain-soaked skin, I felt the deep tears I had not cried when a close friend died. One April, a strong wind brought down from its heights what my father used to call a widow-maker branch. I smiled with the sudden arrival of a long-forgotten memory of how he loved to walk in the woods. Today, I look out, as the setting sun casts the shadow of that tree across newly fallen leaves, and I see more clearly how short life is.

Omens or fortune tellers are unnecessary when you have a tree mirror to project and reflect upon. And a mirror held before the soul makes for a better life.

Singing in a Foreign Land

For there our captors
    asked us for songs,
and our tormentors asked for mirth, saying,
    "Sing us one of the songs of Zion!"
How could we sing the Lord's song
    in a foreign land?

—Psalm 137

Isaac Rogel teaches Spanish to English language speakers. In that capacity he crosses the borders of language and culture easily. What happened one night on a highway in Cuernavaca would force him to cross another border into the foreign land of the differently abled. There he would answer the Psalmist's question by singing a strong new song in celebration of life.

It happened like this. His car broke down on a dangerous highway. He got out and began pushing it out of the traffic. The last thing he remembered was a bright light blinding him. Later, after surviving two heart attacks caused by the trauma and many other life-threatening operations, he learned he had been thrown across the high-speed lanes. Both his legs were crushed and had to be amputated and his right arm was mangled.

Toward the end of his fifteen-month hospital stay, after many more operations and hours of solitude, Isaac found how to sing his song in his new foreign land. From the half-bed that was now his home, he began composing letters to himself. They were letters of honest introspection, addressed to the Isaac within. He began to claim what had not been lost. *Here I am as I am, in my new life,* he wrote. And that statement allowed him to see and accept what he knew must be accepted. After releasing those words he was able to thank God for his life and his friends for their companionship. With a clarity he had not experienced before his arrival in the land of the differently abled, he stated, *I am standing with my face turned to the sky in joyful contemplation, marveling at the wonders of life.*

MY TRUE IDENTITY

Spirit of Life, God of my searching mind, so much of my time is spent trying to discover my true identity. Who am I? What am I to do with my one wonderful and marvelous life? Probing for answers to these questions, I touch the startling truth that the "I" that I seek can only be found in relationship to the pulsing force of life and the people who surround me. The psalmist cried to God saying, "Where can I go from Your spirit, where can I flee from Your presence?" Yet he knew there was no escaping this relationship. And so it is with us. Our true identity is to be found in the relationships we create and is fashioned in the spaces that separate us. Today I pray for the wisdom to live my life, not in isolation, but in the sacred space of togetherness.

RECOGNITION

Spirit of Life, help me see clearly what I am reluctant to recognize in my mirror of self reflection. Open my eyes to my imperfect glory. Such a simple request! Yet I know that I do not know myself, and often fail to acknowledge my strengths and weaknesses. Rumi, your poet of old, once said,

> If you want a clear mirror,
> behold yourself
> and see the shameless truth
> which the mirror reflects.

And so today I will gaze into the mirror of my soul and describe what I see. Tomorrow, strengthened by my honest observations, I will gaze into the mirror others hold up to me and I will say—holy, holy.

COMBUSTION

It's not
the fuel.

It's not
the sparks.

It's the moment
of combustion

when
your passion
for life
burns your soul
into an ember
in the
heart of God.

AMBEDKAR'S CHOICE

Jump into experience while you are alive!
Think . . . and think . . . while you are alive.
What you call "salvation" belongs to the time before death.

—Kabir

Bhimrao Ramji Ambedkar was born in 1891, an "untouch-
able" in India's rigid caste system. He was a member of the
Dalit underclass, situated below the four traditional Hindu
castes. His parents were devotees of the fifteenth-century
Indian poet saint Kabir. Kabir's admonition to *think . . . and*
think was a gift Ambedkar's parents gave to their son. He
used that gift well and eventually earned doctorates from
Columbia University and the University of London. He became one of the most educated persons in India. After India
won independence, Jawaharlal Nehru, the first prime minister, asked Ambedkar to write the nation's constitution.

All his life Ambedkar sought salvation before death for all untouchables. "Educate, Agitate, Organize" became his famous slogan. He sought justice for his people in many ways—as a government official, law school dean, and newspaper editor. He led sit-ins at public and religious sites opposing the treatment of the untouchables. He differed from his contemporary Mohandas Gandhi, not in his commitment to non-violence, but in his analysis that the caste system, not the British Empire, was the greatest barrier to the independence of all India's people.

Ambedkar's passion for justice was interwoven with his quest to find a religion that best represented his belief in human equality. In 1935, after a decade of non-violent resistance to the brutalities suffered daily by the untouchables, Ambedkar announced that he would seek a new religion because he felt that the evils of the caste system could not be separated from traditional Hinduism. He insisted a change in religion was needed to make the world a better place and for individuals to gain self-respect. He said religion had to be a rational choice and that choice had to take into consideration the imperative of justice for all. Requests from religious leaders poured in, urging him to choose their faith tradition. Shortly before his death in 1956 Ambedkar announced he had chosen Buddhism and within a day or two, a half million Hindus converted. Yet, not all Buddhists rejoiced, for with Ambedkar's choice came his interpretation of the core Buddhist teachings. He asserted that his new faith carried a strong imperative to educate, agitate, and organize against injustice. For many Buddhists this approach was unacceptable for it required confrontation and challenge.

For Ambedkar, and for many whose lives burn with a passion for justice, there is a link between the spirit and a religious home to guide and inform their work. Creating that link requires making a conscious choice.

BEING A FORCE OF NATURE

The same stream of life that runs through my veins night and day runs through the world and dances in rhythmic measures.

—Rabindranath Tagore

At the Water's Edge

Spirit of Life, God of my deepest longing, you lure me to the water's edge, where the tide of wonder rises easily into my open heart. Lift my feet over the long meandering rack of washed up certainties that cling to sand made clean by your passing. Here, where winter ice dissolves and sinks deeply into wetlands, where summer foam blows in the wind, and gulls laugh at the sea, I come looking for you. But I don't find you here. When will I learn that your presence is not in a particular place? Anywhere I open my heart I will feel your presence.

Peace Like a River, Strength Like a Mountain

Nature provides ready metaphors for peace and justice. Jesus' peaceful kingdom is described as a mustard seed that grows into a large bush, providing shelter to all. The Hebrew prophet Amos cried for justice to roll down like water, and we sing, "I've got peace like a river" and "strength like a mountain."

But it takes more than mere words to join nature to action. Truly experiencing ourselves as a force of nature in all its varied circumstance is something beyond just symbolism.

The next breath I take is not a metaphor. It is, if I am mindful of it, a reminder that I myself am a force of nature, linked to all that exists on our living, breathing planet. In many American Indian traditions the medicine wheel honors the natural forces that can guide us into harmony with all living things. Our suffering, our victories, and the passions and beliefs that move us to action are part of a larger system that appears at times to seek harmony and at times to tear us apart. In engaging each fully we become forces of nature.

Officials laughed when Wangari Maathai said that the women of her country would plant fifteen million trees. The natural strength of the trees they planted began flowing through the women who planted them and they discovered their own power. Through the simple planting of trees women who lived in poverty and despair began to transform the landscape and themselves. The trees helped reduce soil erosion and water pollution. They provided shade and produced sustainable crops. Wangari Maathai's vision transformed the landscape of Kenya, and the Greenbelt Movement she started has spread to more than thirty countries.

Growing and producing enough food for their families gave Kenyan women a greater vision and unexpected courage. They began to challenge their leaders' dictatorial and environmentally destructive policies. They faced brutal oppression with a strength they could not have imagined when the first trees were planted. *When you plant a tree and you see it grow,* Maathai says, *something happens to you. You want to protect it, and you value it.* The same thing happens with a vision.

GROUNDED

It hurts to let go of intensity
that zapped like electricity
yesterday.

It hurts to disconnect arcing power,
watch it ground and vanish.

What was it that surged through us
to lighten gray, indifferent skies?

What was it that connected
our hearts to hope?

Now we must wait,
for that inward current
to arc us forward again,
connecting our quest for justice
to the power of inner peace.

The Mourning Cloak Butterfly

This is the true joy in life, the being used for a purpose recognized by yourself as a mighty one; the being a force of nature instead of a feverish, selfish little clod of ailments and grievances complaining that the world will not devote itself to making you happy.

—George Bernard Shaw

Matted and torn, thawing brown leaves blanket the ground. Under a quilted patch-work of old wounds and new defeats we rest.

From this landscape a mourning cloak butterfly takes flight. Aptly named, this creature knows something about being a force of nature. It does not fly away or die when winter approaches. In its black cloak trimmed with gold, it waits through the long winter under a blanket of rotting leaves. After a rain, when the world starts turning toward spring, it opens its wings on a rock and is warmed by the sun. Vital energy reenters its body, giving joy to its flight.

We too can push aside the ailments and grievances that bury us, spread our wings toward the light, and let our spirits soar.

In Gratitude

Spirit of eternal gratitude, awaken from your deep resting place in our hearts. In this time when war consumes innocent lives and violence and poverty threaten millions, we pray you will teach us the humble ways of thanksgiving. Help us to remember all who have faced times like these with courage, without false hope or illusions. Today we do not pray for easy victory over the poverty of the soul. We simply thank you for the momentary chance to say yes to life. In the name of all that is sacred, we pray with our hands, our hearts, and our minds for gratitude.

Born of Urgency

A bristlecone pine crawls
out of a seed buried in rocks
above the tree line.
It sets its roots
in star dust,
born from an urgency
that traveled through
dark space
at light speed

until I gazed upon it
and hope and desire
rooted me in the unfinished
work of the universe.

Strength from Silence and a Storm

Rejected and ridiculed by Buddhist leaders for his socially
engaged religious practices, Thich Nhat Hanh and a small
group of like-minded young monks retreated to the forest to
listen to the healing Zen voice of silence. They saw nature
as a Zen koan. The traditional mechanism for a koan is a
pattern of words or stories that, when contemplated, create
space to respond mindfully and correctly to ever-changing
circumstances. Thich Nhat Hanh found truth in nature. The
soothing silence of the forest calmed him; raging storms
were a call from the heart of the cosmos. His response to that
call was a series of bold acts of compassion that directly challenged the government of his own country and of the United
States during the Vietnam War. Decades later, living in much
changed circumstances, he still responds to the cosmos' call.
Wherever you are, there is always the need to listen and
reply to the sound of the universe.

DROPLETS IN RAINBOWS

We awaken, like dewdrops at dawn, clear, sparkling,
filled with morning's glory. Waiting without fear,
we let the rising sun transform us.

At first it seems a physical thing, an attraction
so compelling, so basic, it cannot be resisted.
Tasting its refreshment, savoring its wetness,
desire dissolves and thirst vanishes.

When moist newness and fiery passion meet,
we evaporate into morning mist,
droplets in a rainbow's promise.

HE LOOKED BACK

to live as siblings with beast and flower,
not as oppressors.
—Denise Levertov

Resting on his hind legs, his small body reaching toward the
sun, the chipmunk turned toward me. In my youth, I had
mindlessly hunted many of his kind. But as I watched him
now, I felt a kind of forgiveness in the way he lingered in
my presence, apparently without fear. In that instant, I knew
what I did not know years ago. This delicate child of the
universe was traveling with me on a small green-blue planet
through common space warmed by the sun. Many generations of his kind had come and gone since the first time I
met them in the woods of my youth. Our chance reunion
reminded me that while I had grown up, a new generation of
chipmunks remained to offer me new opportunities to live,
not as oppressor, but as companion with all living things.

VAPORS OF HOPE

I cannot stop it
    breathing in all this
    the carnage of war
    the deep wrenching poverty
    the greed that rests without remorse
    on the still-born dreams of the discarded.

I breathe in
    rancid vapors
    rising from the cities of garbage
    where innocent children play
    and mothers cry for all that is lost.

My lungs ache and my chest heaves.
    Will I drown in all this?
    Will I lose my breath in
    endless waves of war, greed
    and poverty?

Let the vapor of all that has been lost
    rise and mingle
    with the longings of my heart.

Let them collect in me a reservoir of passion
    to flow in currents
    and rise like the mists
    of morning.

I cannot stop breathing, not yet.
    I cannot take it in
    without distilling it
    into fresh air
    then releasing it
    back into the world.

A Certain Comfort

Whatever peace I know rests in the natural world, in feeling myself part of it.

—May Sarton

Water striders use surface tension to glide across the top of water. I have watched these bugs on hot summer days and their patterns of motion have soothed me. Then I saw poet and scientist Loren Eiseley's comments that the film separating the strider from certain death in the water can be broken by a beetle, whose force dissolves the surface tension.

Danger lurks beneath every moment of peace that nature offers. Sit comfortably next to the swaying grasses and the Lyme disease-bearing tick may enter your body, planting seeds of destruction. While watching the gentle roll of the sea, a rogue wave may crash upon you, pulling you under, or worse. The natural world can only provide rest if we honestly understand that the peace it offers comes wrapped in paradox.

Our social institutions too contain built-in dangers to our worth, dignity, and very existence. At the same time they provide the building blocks of human comfort and well-being.

There is a difference between the world of the water strider and beetle and our world. Theirs must be accepted and ours must be tirelessly improved upon. In both, we are left with hope wrapped in contradiction.

The Seed Knows to Grow

Plow following hoof,
machine drilling holes
by rake, by stake
opening the earth.

Collected from eternity
these slender hopes,
cradled on a shaft,

delicately balanced
until only the chosen fall
into brown, black, yellow, red soil.

Freed now, they thrust upward
and push downward.

Placed in rows, ordered in fields
the grain waves
in wind, rain and scorching sun.

Blood soaks the ground
a thousand times,
torrents flow for justice and freedom,
for greed and conquest,
only to nurture the seed.

Tears soak the ground
with sadness and joy.

Sun dries the ground,
collecting anger into clods
and despair into dust.

Weeded, fertilized, harvested,
cut, crushed, sold,
bought and baked,
both sustenance and symbol unit.

We name the gift
praise the tiller, the planter,
the harvester, the baker, the provider.

Yet the seed knows only to grow,
the earth knows only to open,
and we know only to make bread,
bake bread
and give thanks.

Mindful Cutting

I will be the gladdest thing
  Under the sun!
I will touch a hundred flowers
  And not pick one.
    —Edna St. Vincent Millay

The flowers look so beautiful here on my desk—white ones interspersed with colored ones, cascading ones touching tall spiked ones. With each cut to the right height, they speak to me of harmony among diversity. The beauty of each blossom awakens me to the grandeur of nature. What can be wrong with that?

Art instructors warn students of the deadly danger of prolonged unprotected use of certain chemicals that produce spectacular artistic results.

Cutting flowers mindlessly may cause similar long-term damage to the soul. By separating the blossom from the plant and the earth, we may become numb to how our actions can sever the link between earth, sky, and human-kind. A living plant retains that interdependence. Sensing this, Albert Schweitzer told a cautionary tale. A farmer, he said, may rightly cut a thousand flowers while producing feed for his cows. If, however, that same farmer on his way home wantonly cuts the head of a single flower growing on the side of the road, he injures life.

Your Presence

Spirit of Life, God of love, you are forever within me. Your longing for a greater love gave me birth. My fingers feel your touch. When I breathe, you rise in me and lift my heart. When I see the carnage of war or the painful eyes of poverty, your tears flow down my cheeks. Keep me ever-awakened to your presence, so that I too can heal with my touch, lift hearts, and respond to the call of compassion.

EVEN THE ROCKS ARE MOVING

The quiet snow spreads deeply over rocks in my garden. In warmer seasons, sometimes mindlessly, sometimes contritely, I gather them from the nearby woods and place them where they satisfy my spirit. But now, from under the snow, they seem to ask, "Why did you move us here?"

"Who are you to complain?" I say. Rocks, even mountains, have been on the move for ages. Thrust by volcanoes, shoved by frost, moved by deep energy, like homeless travelers they are always on the move.

Come spring my spade will slip into the rich soil beds from which I cleared all rocks last spring. And there I will find new travelers from deep earth. Year after year I cursed their arrival until I understood that all things are on the move and the only real abuse is not to treat them with reverence even while moving them.

A STRANGE BIRD

A bird flew into the woods
 How did he do that? the scientist asks,
 as he flies to the moon
 or makes craters of devastation.

A bird flew into the woods
 Wow! the mystic exclaims,
 and flies beyond the imagination
 or into a lover's arms.

A bird flew into the woods
 and cried
 oh, what a strange bird
 watches me.

PARTICLES OF LOVE

Spirit of Life, God of Love, you radiate the particles of my soul. Sparkling, they spin me free of my ego. Shimmering, they bestow upon me the simple honor of being alive. Shining, they reflect a pathway of humility and service. In the darkness of my own making, remind me that I am a true miracle of this world. Show me the greatness that whirls inside me, undiminished by my excuses and my grand gestures. Let your warmth spread outward from the center of my being until I become a beacon of your radiant love.

NATURE IS NO METAPHOR

We must draw our standards from the natural world. We must honor with the humility of the wise the bounds of that natural world and the mystery which lies beyond them, admitting that there is something in the order of being which evidently exceeds all our competence.

—Vaclav Havel

The chameleon shoots forth its sticky and deadly tongue and the unsuspecting praying mantis dies. Observing this, we conclude that life is cruel and murderous. Then, with a sigh of relief, we watch the behaviors of creatures living in a pride, a pack, or a pod and we see loving affection.

Nature has enough rich variety to support any conclusion we wish to draw from it. We seem incompetent to grasp its full meaning. Beneficial symbiotic relationships and destructive parasitic relationships are all around us.

The conclusions we draw and the metaphors that we create from them, however, are less important than the humility we gain from the encounter itself. Reverently pausing to watch the drama of the chameleon and the mantis, we learn there is something in the order of being that exceeds all our competence.

THE GIFT

The fruitfulness of a gift is the only gratitude for the gift.
                                   —Meister Eckhart

The gift was given, this we know,
    after bursting from a hen's egg—the creator gave it
    after opening a pea pod—the creator gave it
    from the dust of the earth—the creator gave it.

The gift was given, so some say,
    and we came out of the wind cave with
    the prairie dogs, the buffalo, the elk, the deer.

The time was ready, so we came out
    fashioned from this earth,
    for this earth,
    as a gift to this earth
    so we might give back
    the fruit of love
    for this earth.

MAKING SACRED

On a desert expedition, the scientist-priest Pierre Teilhard de Chardin, found himself on a Sunday morning without his sacraments. In a way that satisfied his priestly obligation to say Mass, he took what was at hand and fashioned a holy moment.

Without the symbols of his faith—the bread, the wine, the altar—he proclaimed the whole earth his altar upon which he offered all the labors and sufferings of the world.

Pointing to the rising sun, he said, "Beneath this moving sheet of fire, the living earth wakes and trembles." And into the chalice of his mind, he said, "I shall pour all the sap which is to be pressed out this day from the earth's fruit."

We become a sacred force of nature when we recognize opportunities to create a sacrament from only the elements at hand. Picking courage from the barren ground of oppression, lifting calm from the whirlwinds of rage, holding our wafer-thin egos to the light of truth, we make the moments of our life a living sacrament. Nothing more is needed, nothing less than what we have at hand will do.

WALLS

Something there is that doesn't love a wall,
That wants it down.

—Robert Frost

A borderland is a vague and undetermined place created by the
emotional residue of an unnatural boundary.

—Gloria Anzaldua

Two of its branching arms broke the cedar's fall, forcing its trunk to rest suspended over the remains of an old New England stone wall. Later, at that very spot, a pine crashed full force upon the wall and broke. Neighbors for a long time, this wall and these two dead trees seem to belong together.

This of course was not the wall builder's intent. He had labored hard to remove rocks and trees from the land. He wanted to divide and separate, to clear the trees and construct a wall that would define his pastures, his property, and outline the common lane that passes by my house. When agriculture flourished in this part of the country, the forests were removed and stone walls constructed.

The landscapes of our lives are filled with the residue of unnatural boundaries. Walls built long ago crisscross, separate, and divide long after their purpose has passed. Yet, something there is that doesn't love a wall.

THE RAINBOW SIGN

Whenever I bring clouds over the earth and the rainbow appears
in the clouds, I will remember my covenant between me and you
and all living creatures of every kind.

—Genesis 9:14-15

Perhaps it is true.
One year is a thousand in your sight
perhaps a thousand thousand
and you simply have not seen a rainbow
in a long, long time.

What else would explain it?
The wars, the terror, the torture
flowing from the hands
of men and women
and, yes, even children.

Or, perhaps the rainbow is broken,
fallen into pieces, and now
after a long, long time you
have stopped looking for it.

Perhaps your rainbow was always
only a reflection of our dreams,
our longing for what you
would not or could not give
or have not looked for.

Maybe there is another reason.
Maybe your rainbow
shattered and scattered
and we are its pieces
waiting to be gathered
one by one
and cast against
your cloud-covered sky.

The Scent of the Eternal

The great doors remain closed,
But spring fragrance comes inside anyway,
And no one sees what takes place there.

—Kabir

A dusting of snow covered the road with a reminder that winter was not yet leaving. Unexpectedly, a creature plowed through the old dark snow at curb side. It was on the run and quickly outdistanced me. I watched its black fur move in a sweeping motion from side to side. It was the size of a large fat cat. But this was no ordinary cat, at least not like any I had seen. My flashlight caught white markings on its side as this night traveler undulated down the road. It didn't enter the woods at the end of the road, but made a sharp right turn into my driveway. Slowing down to clear a pile of frozen snow, it proceeded into the garden where I watched it make its distinctive third-rail track into the adjacent woods.

In the house, as I prepared for bed, the creature entered my room. Uninvited, it came in through the small cracks around windows and doors. Its signature walk and tracks were out of sight, but the faint sweet skunk scent penetrated my senses.

Eternal scents of change can arrive in any season of life, even when we have closed the windows and the doors of our heart in anticipation of endless winter. One moment it seems like our soul is frozen; the next, a scent of hope arrives. Even while snow falls, a fellow traveler will join us on a dark road to remind us that what is not yet visible has already arrived. The fresh return of the eternal is a gift of life itself, and it is always waiting for us to sense it. Its power to awaken arrives even when its fragrance is not what we expect.

DISTANT RETURN

Here, I will be discovered and lost:
Here, I will, perhaps, be stone and silence.
           —Pablo Neruda

Someday, out there, on a day like this
in a place I will never see,
where the clearing winds always come
after the storm,
I will arrive nameless
on a distant memory
carrying with me all the best
I gave back to this earth.

All the hope I found
    scattered by others
    along the roads
    I traveled

All the courage that came
    unexpectedly when you took my hand
    and we cried for those
    we could not save

All the love that exposed
    the lies I told myself
    about who I was
    and what I was meant to do

All the faith that came to me
    when I saw others
    carry these things
    into the future.

Winds of Change

They gathered at the edge of my world
whispering, then howling,
then roaring
moving into me
pinning my soul
to this particular place
in this particular position.

Danger spoke loudly in my ear,
"Bend now, bow now
or break."

My heart and mind
spoke back,
"No, not ever."
The winds whirled,
ascending to heaven
crashing down upon me
pushing, shoving,
ripping me open,
spilling all that I had
neatly ordered.

Then the winds were gone.

In the distance
I heard them laughing
as they touched my neighbor
with a gentle evening breeze.

"Wait, wait," I cried.
"Look back here!
Look at what you have done!"

It was too late,
they were gone
and I was left to re-create my world.

ENTWINED

Spirit of Life, God of Love, I am entwined in your delicate web of mutuality. The life energy that makes me reach for the sun also moves me to become wrapped, like the strong bittersweet vine and the delicate sweet pea, around those I meet and love. Here in the tangle of my daily life I feel your pulse and sense what it means to be alive. Here, twisted and knotted, I thrive, seeking the light that will pull from me the fragrant blossom of love. Spirit of Life, help me to experience the beauty of your interwoven and intricate web, that I might always embrace, without reserve, all those whom my life touches.

CONSCIOUS RELATIONSHIPS

Evolution is an ascent toward consciousness.
                    —Teilhard de Chardin

During the summer we enjoyed the frequent plop of a particular frog that lived in a little pond outside our bedroom window. By September it had grown quite large. We attached our hearts to this creature and the familiar sound the water made as it jumped into it. On an early September morning a common garter snake visited the frog's pond. I watched it for a moment then went about my business. A few moments later a song popped into my mind. It was one I sang to our children—"Froggie Went a-Courtin'." The last verse, which I always edited for the children's sake, goes, "Froggie gets eaten by a big green snake." After humming a few bars I quickly went back to the pond. The snake had moved and now the frog's leg was in its mouth. What to do?

Frequently I preach that nature does not care much about the individuals of any particular species. I wondered if I should interfere. Snakes have been eating frogs for a long time. That's the way it is. So I went on with other tasks. But I couldn't get the drama out of my head. How could I? I had a relationship with this frog and only moments ago looked it in the eye while its leg was in the mouth of a snake. This wasn't a frog living in a song or a distant pond being eaten by some hypothetical snake. This was the frog whose plop had brought a smile to my face many times as I woke in the morning or went to bed at night. At that moment I decided to intervene somehow. Let that old snake, I thought, eat some out-of-sight frog.

When I arrived back at the pond the frog was sitting on the rock—all alone—and the snake was gone. I sighed with relief and pleasure that I had decided to be a force of nature and ascended enough toward self-consciousness to act to save a relationship rather than do nothing.

LIBERATING ENERGY

With a powerful flutter of its tiny wings an immature thrush struggled in a trap I had unintentionally devised. Years before I had carefully strung the chicken wire between two compost bins behind the garage. Now, in its first season of life, a tiny bird struggled to free itself from the wire.

I approached the bins unaware of what I'd done, my mind focused on the graceful landing of a red-tailed hawk nearby. Then, suddenly I heard the frantic flutter of the little bird. Before I could fully grasp the situation and devise a liberation strategy, the bird intensified its efforts and broke free.

In the midst of struggle we sometimes think we are making every possible effort to free ourselves from this habit or that situation—only to discover that the liberating energy we need to set us free still lies within.

In the Intervals

We grow up; but the earth remains a child.
Star and flowers, in silence, watch us go.
—Rainer Maria Rilke

I know a place where in glorious intervals life is eternally new. You come to it through a young wood where pine and oak grow tall. You'll know you are close when you bend under a weathered cedar and, as you straighten your back, you see the elephant skin of a ancient copper beech.

From the woodland path you can see a river of low growth whose surface is slightly over your head. If you follow the flow down stream, birds will delight you as your footsteps set them in fearful flight. At the top of a knoll, just off the path, I have thrown my body out to dry on warm flat ledge rocks. You can see marsh grass from that ledge. In early spring the ice, like dirty meringue, sticks against the muddy path. There, on shrub-size willows, red-winged blackbirds puff their chests and trill at arriving newness. On branches just within reach, thrushes build their nests.

If you look closely at the base of those willows you will see twisted and torn stumps the size of the shoots that are now balancing new life. On a misty morning, after the rain has stopped, you can hear blackbirds singing several octaves below the sizzling hum of the high-tension electric lines.

The electric lines must be protected from growing things, so every five years an army of cutting machines marches out to sweep away the blackbird perches and thrushes' nests.

In my living room I have a remnant of the last time the great cutting machines paraded in formations. It is a thin twisted trunk of a young willow. I have decorated it with an altar cloth of red leaves from a creeping vine that grows over the ledge where I rest.

We live in intervals between cuttings. In the time that we are blessed to grow, let our music rise like the song birds. Let us affirm the earth's way of seeing the world as a child.

Eternal Currency

But, what about love?
Does love have eternal currency?

Will my love for you become valueless when I die?
Will it be buried forever,
    lost when the pictures of us on the piano
    no longer sing our song,
    lost to some distant, not-yet-born relative
    who discovers us smiling in that picture
    we placed in a book of love poems?

What about my love-driven actions
    with the poor, the oppressed and abused?
Will they rest in bins of memorabilia
    of campaigns won and lost?
Will what I did with him or her or them
    wash away like sacrificial blood?

Perhaps love is not a currency at all.
Perhaps it is just there
    like air or water
    to be used, and used
    and used again.

Rhythms of Change

Spirit of the changing seasons, I trust and delight in the certainty that each change you make, no matter how wrenching, brings the promise of new life. Yet, in the affairs of my own life, I have no such confidence. Moments of chaos can easily lead to despair and hopelessness. In troubled times I pray that dawn follows the night and spring arrives after winter has lingered too long. In the uncertainty of such moments, help me accept change with the delight of a child coming of age or an elder embracing new-found wisdom. When I long for the comforts of what can no longer be, lift my head above my losses and fears and cast my eyes on the promise of new beginnings.

This Sacred Place

This place has been waiting for us,

> *To gather our dreams*
> *of justice and peace.*

This place has been waiting for us,

> *To honor it by opening our hearts*
> *and speaking our minds.*

This place has been waiting for us,

> *To fill it with compassion*
> *and loving kindness.*

This place has been waiting for us,

> *To draw from it a breath*
> *of common purpose.*

This place has been waiting for us,

> *To listen to the wisdom of its silence.*

This place has been waiting for us,

> *To fill it with the urgency*
> *of new possibilities.*

This place has been waiting for us,

> *To make it sacred*
> *by our coming together.*

Seasonal Blessings

Spirit of Life, God of my unfolding life, help me to welcome this new day. Let me rest in my winter until I feel the sun lift my edges, pulling open my frozen tightness. Let me feel the rushing warmth necessary to complete the gesture. In the lengthening days, when my surfaces shimmer in rising currents of air and quiver in evening breezes, revitalize me and soothe me with simple stillness. When the harvest ends the cycle, grant me the wisdom to let go of all that has passed. I pray that these seasonal blessings will make me flexible enough to gracefully bow earthward in the storm and supple enough to withstand the brittle thirst of draught. On the edge of each new day, grant me the wisdom to accept the changes that arrive, and the insight to know that the human heart seldom has seasons as predictable as those brought by the turning of the earth.

Being a Force of History

Nothing true or beautiful or good makes complete sense in any immediate context of history; therefore, we are saved by faith.

—Reinhold Niebuhr

BE THE CHANGE

After four decades of study and writing, Will and Ariel Durant completed their ten-volume *The Story of Civilization*. Later, in a thin book entitled *The Lessons of History* they offered this observation: "History is so indifferently rich that a case for almost any conclusion from it can be made by selecting instances."

I once found this notion unsettling. Certainly, I thought, history was on the side of the righteous ones, like myself. I reached freely into history's deep pockets to prove my points. I did this with a conviction fearfully similar to those who argue that God is on their side.

But now I agree that it's not possible to find objective truth in history. No one can say with complete confidence and honesty that history is on her side. At the same time, those who want to move the world in the direction of equality and lasting harmony must become, and learn to think of themselves as, forces of history.

In a world of clashing and conflicting definitions, it matters tremendously when we declare ourselves willing to be judged as partisans for a particular cause. No one possesses the whole truth or can predict where his actions will lead, but to do nothing is to add one more problem to the troublesome equation. In this regard, being a force of history requires both humility and courage.

Mohandas Gandhi was one of the twentieth century's most powerful forces of history. He accepted his time and place, religiously practiced self reflection in his Hindu tradition, and had the courage to confront the greatest empire on earth with the power of non-violence. The movement he shaped brought independence to India.

Gandhi extracted moral truth from the vast complexities of India's history and presented it as an imperative for non-violent action by individuals. "Be the change you seek," he taught, and a nation and the world listened.

Saving the World

When society is made up of men who know no interior solitude
it can no longer be held together by love: and consequently it is
held together by a violent and abusive authority.

—Thomas Merton

We have only begun to know
the power that is in us if we would join
our solitudes in the communion of struggle.

—Denise Levertov

In October 1961 the world held its breath. The Soviets had placed nuclear capable missiles in Cuba. President Kennedy's military advisors wanted a quick military response including air strikes and an invasion. Fearing an irrational response, the President instead established a naval blockade. The Soviets publicly stated that they would remove missiles from Cuba if the United States removed its missiles from Turkey. The crisis grew more acute when a U.S. spy plane was shot down over Cuba and the pilot killed. The world was at the brink of nuclear war.

At a crucial point in the crisis, Acting Secretary General of the United Nations U Thant proposed several actions: a standstill on both sides, continued negotiations, and the possible removal of U.S. weapons from Turkey. These proposals allowed the superpowers to disengage and the world to breathe again.

U Thant's spiritual strength is often overlooked in this story. He brought to the crisis his well-practiced diplomatic skills, rooted in his daily spiritual practice of meditation, prayer, contemplation, self searching, and questioning. These he believed linked the individual life to the universe. His practice was based on mindfulness and treating each individual with the utmost care and kindness.

One key factor that saved the world from nuclear war in October 1961 was the presence of a single man whose spiritual practice linked his interior solitude with his public practice of caring for others.

GENERATION TO GENERATION

Lord, you have been our dwelling place
throughout all generations.

—Psalm 90

In April 1933 Julie Bonhoeffer was ninety years old. The Nazi Party had transformed her homeland and imprisoned the principles of her church. With the strength of her Christian faith she defied a Nazi boycott of Jewish businesses and walked through a gauntlet of brownshirts to buy strawberries from forbidden merchants.

Three years later her grandson, the renowned theologian and author Dietrich Bonhoeffer, eulogized his grandmother. "We can no longer think about our own lives," he said, "without thinking of hers. She belongs entirely to us and will always do so."

The breadth and width of history can be overwhelming. It can diminish us as certainly as does looking at the galaxies from our home on the edge of the Milky Way. Our minds fumble as we try to grasp the significance of our actions here at the front line of human achievement and failure.

History, however, is only the sequence of moments lived. What we do and fail to do shape the lives and deaths of others. The psalmist's refrain, *from generation to generation*, reminds us that we are the guardians of the best humankind has claimed from history. Dietrich Bonhoeffer, for all his accomplishments as an interpreter of the Christian faith, is remembered most for the courage he inherited from his grandmother. He died in a Gestapo prison for his efforts to bring down the Nazi regime.

Memories of hope, courage, and love are our dwelling place from generation to generation.

Time-Location

There is no choice but to immerse oneself in the stream of history, accept one's time-location, breathe in—with shared memories and hopes—the contamination of tradition, become defined as the man of this cause, this party, this emergency.
—William Ernest Hocking

Being a force of history and a lover of life at the same time can feel like an uneasy combination. When we are forces of history we engage with the problems of the world and act to improve on them. But as lovers of life we delight in mere existence—the beauty of watching a bird in flight or the light fading into dusk. As Rumi points out: the lover is always getting lost and choosing to drown in the eternal. Must we choose between immersing in the issues of the day and drowning in love?

Two arts are required: to *get lost* in love and *accept one's time-location.* Like Rumi's Dervishes, we are compelled to whirl in love—holding one hand toward the heavens and one hand toward the earth. Grounded in this way, we are moved to engage history with hope and push it toward a more just future.

Perhaps practicing the two arts is like taking a breath. Breathe in the deeds of history and breathe out the joy of living. Breathe in the joy of living and breathe out the deeds of history.

Give Me the Strength

Spirit of my longing heart, help me become a force of history. Like a drop of water let me merge and mingle in the currents of my particular time and situation and not hold back, but join what nurtures the earth and soaks the seeds of justice and peace. Let me be the flash point where the light begins to travel at great speed, igniting compassion, that others might see the power of goodness. Let me rush with the winds of change across the desolate plains of greed and selfish desire. Grant me the wisdom to know that the winds of eternal hope blow through my words and deeds. Let me join the sky with its watchful eye and be a witness to life affirmations wherever I see them. Give me the strength to say yes to even the smallest act of mercy. With these powers of earth, of light, of wind, of sky, I will change myself and become a gift of love and power to the story of humankind.

SPIRITUAL DIMENSIONS OF A LIFE

I saw the holy city, the new Jerusalem, coming down out of heaven . . . The city lies four square . . . its length and width and height are equal.

— Revelation 21

The writer of this passage looks out from his prison cell and sees a vision that gives him hope. Martin Luther King Jr. had an affinity for this passage even before his beliefs led him to prison. He preached from this text while addressing the Dexter Avenue Baptist Church in Montgomery as its ministerial candidate. He used it again years later when preaching at St. Paul's Cathedral in London on his way to accept the Nobel Peace Prize. His message on both occasions was that an individual life, like the new Jerusalem, has equal dimensions of length, breadth, and height. For Dr. King the length was an individual's essential worth and dignity, the breadth was his relationship to and responsibility for the welfare of others, and the height was a personal relationship with God.

Unlike the imprisoned writer of old, too often we only see one- or two-dimensional visions. Such distortions lead to false measurements of who we are and what we can contribute to the world. As a result our lives become lopsided, sometimes painfully so. Balanced and carefully developed, however, the spiritual dimension of our lives can, as Dr. King argued, keep us balanced and change the world.

IMPATIENCE

Impatience grows in me,
I am a roaring river,
denouncing ignorance and innocence.
I race on
with rapid judgments.

Impatience grows in me,
I am a lava flow,
melting reasoned indifference.
I race on
with hot passions.

Impatience grows in me,
I am a whirlwind,
churning up forgotten hopes.
I race on
with frightening momentum.

Impatience, impatience
grows in me,
tiring my body.
Impatience throws my dreams,
one by one,
deep into the earth
where I watch them
languishing, dying
until I pick them up.
I pick them up
and reshape them with
patience, passion
and possibility.

MAKING MEANING

Has life a "meaning"? Experience life as reality and the question becomes meaningless.

—Dag Hammarskjöld

Dag Hammarskjöld lived a life of action. As an economist he coined the term *planned economy* and through legislation gave it shape in his native Sweden. His diplomatic skills led him to the United Nations, where he was twice elected Secretary General. He practiced what he called "preventive diplomacy" on three continents and his work set the standards and procedures for the UN's initial peace-keeping efforts.

Throughout his life Hammarskjöld kept a journal. This, he said, was "a sort of White Book concerning my negotiations with myself—and with God." His journal writing was about meaning making—the meaning of his personal reality. It kept him focused and humble. "You are not the oil," he wrote to himself, "you are not the air—merely the point of combustion, the flash point where the light is born."

To find meaning we must become a means and not an end—*a flash point of combustion.* We engage in self-reflection to see the world in ways that help us be the point where the light is born.

REVERENCE FOR LIFE

Reverence for life comprises the whole ethic of love in its deepest and highest sense. It is the source of constant renewal for the individual and for mankind.

—Albert Schweitzer

Traveling upriver on an errand of mercy, Albert Schweitzer could not focus his thoughts. An acclaimed theologian and physician, he was having difficulty grasping the link between nature and ethics. Then the words *reverence for life* flashed across his mind, sweeping away all rational complexities.

"If you study life deeply," Schweitzer said, "looking with perceptive eyes into the vast animated chaos of this creation, its profundity will seize you suddenly with dizziness." That dizziness led him to leave his successful career as a theologian and musician to study medicine and then abandon his comfortable life in Europe to create a small village hospital in Africa.

The ethic of love, embedded in the natural world and in our very souls, is waiting to seize us with a dizziness so that we can accomplish the unimaginable.

WHEN THE PAST ARRIVES

Gather what you can for we must leave now.
Gather what you must,
for hatred is marching
and we are no longer safe.

What shall we take? Time is running out.
The way from here will be rough
and we'll make justice as we go.

Take only what you can carry.

"Carry me," history cries.
From her wrinkled mouth
she begs, "Carry me lightly in your hearts."

Gather what you can into your hearts
the present moment has arrived
and we must leave much behind.

Peace for All

No task is more important to me than promoting the well-being of all the people.

—Asoka Edicts (ca. 274-232 BCE)

Victorious, but with a heavy heart, King Asoka looked out over the battlefield of Kalinga, a Kingdom he would now annex to form his vast empire. He was the third Emperor of the Maurya dynasty and he ruled most of the Indian subcontinent.

Asoka was moved to deep sorrow by the carnage he had inflicted and the sight of 100,000 dead and 150,000 taken into captivity. In his meditation on the horror of what he saw he mentioned the burning stick of anger that his Buddhist tradition warned against holding.

Asoka spent the rest of his life teaching that insight into oneself and respect for others were the essence of both religion and politics. He ordered his life, his royal household, and his kingdom by the Buddhist precepts of loving kindness, compassion, empathic joy, and equanimity. Edicts conveying these truths were carved in stone and placed throughout the land and at its borders. All religions were honored in his kingdom. Asoka's reign reflected his belief that moral practice could be elevated through meditation and insight.

A change of heart can change the course of a life and of history. It can move us to erect noble tablets at the borders of all we say and do.

It's a Great Day to Be Alive

Predictably, Mildred would say these words as she welcomed me—"It's a great day to be alive and it's good to be here with you." It was a simple enough greeting to be forgotten, but it has stayed with me for many decades now. The reason it lives with me today is because Mildred was a hope-giver.

Mildred Scott Olmstead was known for her leadership in the peace and justice movements of her time. She was the first director of the U.S. chapter of the Women's International League for Peace and Justice. She worked with Jane Addams to found that organization and became its director after returning from her service as a social worker in Europe during the First World War.

Her blue eyes sparkled when she told of campaigns won and lost. But Mildred did not live in all that rich history she experienced. Even in her nineties she wanted to talk about the news of the day. Today, she thought, was always a "great day to be alive." She seemed to know that now is the only time to influence the future. When I would recite a litany of losses that our common causes had suffered, she would say "those who oppose women's rights and peace should be quaking in their boots." At the time her confidence seemed ill-founded to me. But she was undaunted and hopeful. This, I believe, came from years of championing seemingly lost causes only to watch others pick up the faltering banners and carry them into the future. As she grew older she seemed to know what Reinhold Niebuhr said so well: Nothing worth doing can be completed in one life.

ACTION MATTERS

Spirit of Life, God of Love, how long can we live with the pain of not knowing what to do? How long will we use complexity as an excuse to do nothing? When will we stop letting analysis and cynicism paralyze and demoralize us? What knowledge must we gain to do what needs to be done? We turn the future into needless suffering with our inaction.

Eternal Spirit of Hope, from time to time you present us with someone who speaks a simple truth: "People who have food, shelter, and healing medicine must learn to share, that is all." God of Love, guide us to the knowledge that moves our inert hands to action. Show us how to use them to build a future of hope.

Rejoice

When the victor cries for all the dead,

Then my heart will rejoice.

When the vanquished forget vengeance,

Then my heart will rejoice.

When the greedy share their wealth,

Then my heart will rejoice.

When the indifferent act with courage,

Then my heart will rejoice.

When success is ours, and ours means everyone's,

Then my heart will rejoice.

Anticipating this,

I will rejoice in shaping victories of love.

Anticipating this,

I will rejoice in creating triumphs of forgiveness.

Anticipating this,

*I will rejoice in sharing my wealth
and the fruits of my labor.*

Anticipating this,

*I will call you my sister
and you my brother.*

Anticipating this,

We will clasp hands in common struggle.

ARMED FOR CONFLICT

When injustice threatened our innocence,
we clamped down our breastplates of certainty,
protected hearts aching for justice.

We put on righteousness
as a coat of armor,
sharpened angry words,
thrust spears of judgment.

After the battles we
counted our casualties,
mourned our losses,
then cried,
"Peace, peace."

And there was no peace.

CROSSING BORDERS

Spirit of my longing and lonely heart, help me travel through
the barren borderlands that separate me from others. Teach
me to willingly explore relationships with those who frighten
or threaten me, grant me the courage to risk confidently my
own comforts, that I might make others more comfortable.
And when I am burdened by the isolating choices I have
made, grant me the wisdom to invite a stranger to travel with
me. Open my heart to my new companion's needs and desires
until I relax my defensiveness and become a calming presence. As we travel, grant me the vision to notice how each
step we take together moves us closer to the promised land,
where all souls grow in hope and the resilience of love.

My Saints

For all the saints whose perfections and imperfections have shaped my life, I give thanks. Some have traveled with me a long time and witnessed the best and the worst I have offered the world. Others have been with me only briefly. Among these traveling companions are those who have died, but have not vanished. Sometimes they arrive unexpectedly in the middle of my busy days and ask what I'm doing and why. In quiet moments they come to rest in the inner-most part of my soul, telling me I am not alone. Sometimes they arrive as ghosts of my unfinished business. Floating freely through closed doors, they unlock my certainties to remind me of what I did or failed to do for others. My saints don't perform miracles with bags of magic tricks. Rather, they are transformers who change my life.

They arrive to comfort me with love, challenge me with truth, or confront me with what needs doing. In the days ahead, I pray that I will have the courage to welcome the wisdom all my saints bring.

Change with Charity

Somewhere in my attic is a handsomely framed piece of art from a long-forgotten campaign to establish new national spending priorities. Its reds, greens, and blues are still bold and exciting, but its white background has yellowed. The hand-written message reads: *Change not Charity.* Looking back on this sign now, I agree—in a truly just world there would be no need for charity; the wealth would be distributed fairly. But, standing alone, this phrase is dangerous if it diminishes the value of bold acts of compassion that ease suffering.

Why do we compare, contrast, and categorize to make our point, to justify our actions?

What advantage can there be in separating bold acts of compassion from passionate cries for reform and transformation? This kind of thinking divides the chambers of the heart and damages the soul.

The Samaritan, a solitary figure in the familiar story told by Jesus, crosses the road of hatred and indifference to help another. After caring for the beaten man, he charitably pays for his continued care. Such courageous acts are life-giving. And they do not diminish the need to rebuild the dangerous Jericho Road. New roads take time to build and we can't leave behind those travelers who have been beaten and robbed by injustice.

PRIVILEGE

I am of the opinion my life belongs to the whole community and as long as I live it is my privilege to do for it what I can.
—George Bernard Shaw

They welcomed me as an honored guest and showed me a comfortably decorated room. With loving voices they told how they had renovated this space for their aging parents. Speaking almost in unison they said softly to each other, "What a privilege it was to provide for them."

Giving freely to help parents is not uncommon, but extending that privilege to serve the broader community is. The next morning as my hosts drove me to my speaking engagement they made a brief, matter-of-fact comment that I have carried with me for years. Speaking of a recently defeated city tax proposal they said, "Our parents taught us that it was a privilege to pay taxes for the good of the community."

The abundant heart does not consider service a punishment or sharing a burden. Rather, it sees the unmet needs of the community as if they were those of a loved one and acts to meet them.

Is That Not Enough?

Spirit of Life, God of our long-suffering lives, you were there when we stumbled and lay trembling as our tormentors cheered. You were there when we lived with unfounded fears. We heard you crying and moaning with us when we were defeated by our own hand and conquered by our own imagination.

When we asked, where is our savior? You, with your patience waning, sighed: *I will always be with you. Is that not enough? What more do you want to know than that I will be with you when others wound you and you damage your own soul?*

Before our hearts turn to despair and self-serving pity, lift from us all illusions. Grant us the wisdom to say of each moment—it is enough.

We the People

Spirit of life, God of love, my heart is moved by the passions of those who crafted dreams of democracy and the rule of law out of chaos. While still clinging to slavery and the special rights of men and of property, they looked deeply into the well of wisdom and saw that humanity was one and proclaimed, "We the people." Today fear, greed, and the assertion that "might makes right" threaten to divide the people of this planet.

I pray for the courage to let my life bear witness to the power of "we"—the people of this nation and this earth. When I am afraid to speak or act for the benefit of all, show me the beauty and power of courage. When I am tempted to abandon the common good for the glory and enrichment of myself, show me the virtue of selfless generosity and hospitality. And when by sure power or will I would claim the right to diminish the worth and dignity of others, grant me the wisdom of humility.

Vanishing Song Birds

*I understand history as possibility . . . that could also stop being
a possibility.*

—Paulo Freire

The winds of extinction sing a mournful song
to the rustling grass,
where the bobwhite drums
and the meadowlark's melody
is vanishing.

The winds of extinction sing a mournful song
in the dark forest shadows,
where the boreal chickadee's
voice is no longer heard
and the grosbeak
serenades a coming hush.

The winds of extinction sing a mournful song
over the troubled waters,
where the great scaup
quietly rests for the last time
and the harsh-voiced tern
skydives to death.

The winds of extinction sing a mournful song
while we wait
to find our voices
to sing for their rebirth.

Distillations

Boil your passions for justice,
boil your longings for peace.
Let them rise in dream-vapors,
condensing
what you seek.

Redefining Courage

Nothing less than a great daring in the face of overwhelming odds can achieve the inner security in which fear cannot possibly survive.

—Howard Thurman

War and hunting were a way of life for the Crow people. Then the beaver and the buffalo were killed by those who hunted for more than food and warmth. Then the warring between the tribes was banished by those who knew other ways to kill their enemies. Then the land was taken by those who thought they could own it.

Crow Chief Plenty Coups grew up during this transition and became a great hunter and warrior. He was fearless and his people followed him. But how could he lead now that hunting and tribal warfare no longer defined courage and leadership?

A vision dream Plenty Coups had at the age of nine provided him with a radically new source of courage and hope. He would need to become fearless in a different way. In his dream the buffalo were gone and the Four Winds waged war on the forest. After the war only one tree was left standing and in that tree was the lodge of the Chickadee. A voice in his dream spoke to him: "The Chickadee is least in strength but strongest of mind among his kind. He is willing to work for wisdom. The Chickadee-person is a good listener. It is the mind that leads to power, not strength of body."

Plenty Coups would never again plant his coup stick as a sign of courage. He would never again lead the great hunts. He would acknowledge that his people's way of life, with all its defined meanings and values, was gone forever. As he moved into the unknown and frightening future, he followed the way of the Chickadee. Seeking wisdom and listening became the test of his courage to lead.

LEADERSHIP

There is simply a point at which social analysis must be validated in action or else it becomes morbid, self-indulgent, and misleading, compounding the very issues it professes to clarify.
—William Stringfellow

William Winpisinger lived at the heart of what President Eisenhower called the military-industrial-complex. He was the president of the International Association of Machinists and Aerospace Workers Union, that represented many employees of defense contractors. In an interview for my radio program, I asked him, "Why have you broken ranks with other union leaders to oppose increases in military spending? Aren't you concerned that many of your members will lose their jobs?" His animated response was filled with facts and analysis. A large portion of the military budget, he said, was going to a few, highly paid scientists, corporate executives, and investors. Relatively little went to pay his workers or to improve national defense. These facts convinced him that the ethical thing to do was to lobby for reductions in military spending. Then, with a firm voice, he said, "All the facts are in, all the studies have been made, it is time to get on with the business of doing the right thing."

Analysis can provide ethical clarity or it can be misleading, compounding the very issues it professes to explain. Ethical leadership requires analysis that clarifies and action that validates.

FEARING GREATNESS

Hour by hour, day by day, the world sets before us false images of greatness. Ideas of wealth and fame flood our minds. Pictures of ideal families, bodies, and work set us to longing. We take them into our hearts and quickly conclude that we are not great. We bow our heads in fear and shame before these false gods. Trembling, we lay aside the limp image of our true self, the one that was a gift from our beginning.

The poet Maya Angelou says that the day of peacemaking will only arrive after we affirm that we are miraculous and the true wonder of this world. Why do we not accept the greatness that has been bestowed upon us?

Remembering September 11

O let America be America again—
The land that has never been yet—
And yet must be . . .
                    —Langston Hughes

Into gray clouds where everyday living vanished,
where every breath burned and every odor offended,
beyond limits of endurance and above duty, they went.

Husbands, wives, sons, daughters,
grandfathers and grandmothers
risking themselves, giving back
to a nation of decadent isolation
the notion of we the people.

Onto steel, concrete, fire and water
they deliberately placed their steps.
Again and again, after praying
over the dead and wounded,
they, the Christian, the Muslim, the Humanist,
the Buddhist, the Agnostic, the Jew,
they, the Americans—the Native- the Asian- the African-
stepped together into
the land of the free and the home of the brave.
Courage, compassion, and commitment rose
from the ashes that day
as they, in their daily routines of care and protection,
they, who never received
signing bonuses or golden parachutes,
became our heroes and showed us who we the people
yet must be.

UP TO A POINT

For everything there is a season, and a time for every matter
under heaven

—Ecclesiastes 3:1

I believe you, up to a point.

The seasons of my life flow with a certain predictability.
I was born and I will die—
I have laughed and I have cried—
I have reaped and I have sown.

Had you stopped there, I could believe all you had to say.

But you went too far with your seasonal metaphor,
with your quest to prove that there is
nothing new under the sun
and all will be the same forever and ever.

What were you thinking when you said there is
a time to love, and a time to hate,
a time for war, and a time for peace?

Is there ever a time to hate?
Or a time to stop loving the children
and give them up to war?
What about the parents who reap and walk home
to hungry children?

Clearly you have confused
the inevitable with the unacceptable.

That's why I will believe you,
up to a point.

THE MEANING OF SUFFERING

To this day, I cannot forget those who suffered with me and died in that clandestine prison. In spite of the humiliation that demanding answers has entailed, I stand with the Guatemalan people. I demand the right to a future built on truth and justice.

—Dianna Ortiz

Dianna Ortiz is an American, an Ursuline nun who taught children in the western highlands of Guatemala. In 1989, she was accused of being a guerilla and conspiring against the Guatemalan government, imprisoned, and tortured. While being tortured she heard the voice of an American, the trainer of her tormentors.

Dianna was freed after the American trainer realized she was not just another helpless Guatemalan woman but an American nun who might expose the involvement of the U.S. government in torture. In Guatemala during this time thousands of civilians repeatedly suffered as Dianna did.

Realizing that her voice might be heard, Dianna, traumatized and suffering, brought charges against the Guatemalan government and told her story to U.S. Department of Justice investigators. Both governments responded with repeated threats, intimidation, and misinformation. Those who treated her so cruelly were never brought to justice, nor was the American trainer ever identified. After four years the Organization of American States, the world's oldest regional organization representing 34 countries, confirmed that she had been tortured and her honor and reputation maligned. Even though justice was never served and the United States was never officially found guilty of training torturers, Dianna's act of speaking truth to power brought meaning to her suffering.

Victor Frankl, whose suffering in a Nazi concentration camp informed his later writings, observed: *Whenever one is confronted with an inescapable, unavoidable situation, whenever one has to face a fate that cannot be changed . . . what matters above all is the attitude we take toward suffering, the attitude in which we take our suffering upon ourselves.*

In our daily lives few of us face the brutality Ortiz and Frankl experienced, yet we often suffer from the realization that certain circumstances cannot change and that we, no matter how willful and skillful, are not in control. At such moments speaking truth can be the most powerful way to give meaning to our suffering.

Now

Don't tell me now is not the time to care for the young,

Just because you're old.

Don't tell me now is not the time to care for the elderly,

Just because you're young.

Don't tell me now is not the time to feed my baby,

Just because you're not hungry.

Don't tell me now is not the time to go to the hospital,

Just because you're feeling fine.

Don't tell me now is not the time to buy new books,

Just because you've read yours.

Don't tell me now is not the time to open the shelter,

Just because you've gone home.

Don't tell me now is not the time to hire,

Just because your investments are weak.

Don't tell me now is not the time to build new bridges,

Just because you've crossed over.

PRACTICE

If you build castles in the air, your dreams need not be lost, that is where they should be. Now put foundations under them.

—Henry David Thoreau

BALANCE

Keeping physically and spiritually balanced, while the whirl-winds of anger and oppression rage, requires us to discipline our bodies, minds, and spirits.

The Dalai Lama says his daily reflections on the Bodhisattva vows help him clear away the burden he sometimes feels concerning the oppression in his homeland of Tibet. Every day he prays:

As long as the sky exists
And as long as there are sentient beings,
May I remain to help
Relieve them of all their pain.

The pacifist A.J. Mustie once said, "There is no way to peace, peace is the way." As a young seminarian I was honored to sit in a small class with Rev. Mustie. His words did not penetrate my soul until much later when I remembered what he said about "being peace," especially when you feel anger building toward the war-makers. Practice is the only way. William Sloane Coffin once said, "All the troubled waters in the world cannot sink your ship unless you let them inside your soul."

Memorizing scriptures, poetic words, songs, and sermons have often helped me maintain or regain my balance. Physical disciplines such as Yoga and Tai Chi can also help maintain equilibrium. Thich Nhat Hanh first used the term "engaged Buddhism" to describe a new kind of social activism. He believes that even the simplest thing, like a practiced smile, can help assure the continued practice of what he calls *lovingkindness* when we are confronted with anger and hatred. That is why he chose the words "A Manual on Meditation for the Use of Young Activists" as the original subtitle of his widely popular book *The Miracle of Mindfulness.*

Motions of words, deeds, silence, and song can be just the practice we need to keep us upright when the world around us lies in ruins.

AMONG THE FLAGS

We have gathered here among the flags,

> *To remember all that has been lost and all that has been gained by the death of these men and women.*

We have gathered here, young and old, liberal and conservative, those who believe these deaths were necessary and those who believe otherwise.

> *Each of us brings to this moment the remnants of our own life's journey, our own experiences with death and dying, our experiences with war and peace, and the meaning we have extracted from them.*

Some of us have traveled through other wars, some through non-violent struggles for peace, and still others have traveled through personal trials that have cost them their innocence.

> *Each of us comes here to this field of flags, where death is no abstraction and where none of us dares judge the motives and assumptions of another.*

Here, whatever our beliefs, we stop to cry for the loss of those these flags represent.

> *We cry for those left behind, who must gather meaning from grief and hope from pain and despair.*

Here we remember the courage of those who have died.

> *May we learn from them so that we might live in the face of our own fears and live more freely.*

Here we remember their commitment to a greater good.

> *May we learn from them what it means to live unselfishly for the common good.*

Here we remember the glory of self-sacrifice in the name of ideals that transcend our individual lives and particular ideologies.

May we take from their glory what we need to transcend small and self serving goals.

Here we remember that those who have died need not have died in vain.

On the altar of our broken hearts we pledge our allegiance to the dawning of a new day when we, the children of this earth, no longer find it necessary to go to war.

In the name of all that is holy, may it be so.

BE HAPPY

People want you to be happy. Don't keep serving them your pain.
                                                              —Rumi

The eyes of a child in a soup kitchen reflect the poverty of our resolve. The silence of a soldier's flag-draped coffin echoes our faint cries for peace, and every global-warming breeze whispers of our greed and selfishness. Anywhere we look we can see injustice and war.

Seven hundred years ago there was no less pain than there is today. At the time of Rumi's birth, Genghis Khan and his armies moved westward, conquering and brutalizing everyone in their path. Rumi's family escaped, yet war, injustice, and uncertainty were never far off. Amidst all this, the Sufi scholar and teacher chose to whirl from his dervish soul a deep joy of life and a mystical love of God. Rumi sought union with the beloved god of his understanding. His prescription for happiness was quite simple—untie your wings and free your soul of jealousy.

Vow Making

Come, come, whoever you are,
Wanderer, worshiper, lover of leaving
This is not a Caravan of despair.
It doesn't matter that you've broken
Your vows a thousand times, still
Come, and yet again, come.

—Rumi

Taking vows seems a quaint idea. Pledging to live better lives in service to others is almost obsolete. Even the powerful lines "till death do us part" are often said with fingers crossed.

Jewish philosopher Martin Buber observed that we are a promise-making, promise-breaking, and promise-keeping people. This, he said, is the part of the human condition that puts us in relationship with others and with God.

Perhaps we have lost our interest in promising because we do not believe that it will do any good for ourselves or others. Perhaps we believe promising might help, but are afraid to risk who we are for who we might become.

Come, Come. Keep on promising, knowing that you will break your vows a thousand times. *Come, Come* is a summons to a better self, a better life, and a better world.

What to Grow

The events of a single day strike a full balance. At any moment enough evidence might be presented to convince us that evil will soon rule the world. In the next moment we may see people breaking free from their fears, confessing the hurt they have caused others, and asking for forgiveness. In such a moment we might think love will win. Life offers both the sweet blueberry and the poisonous nightshade. Both are real, both grow when given the right conditions. Our moment-to-moment task is not to deny the nature of growing things, but to choose what we will grow in our garden.

THE HALF-SMILE

(in gratitude for Thich Nhat Hanh's practice)

It will be hard
on a day like this.
After so much,
who would blame you
for abandoning your practice?

You have seen
war and deep poverty,
faces robbed of resilience,
eyes drained of hope,
brows plowed with anger,
and mouths frozen in sadness.

Yet, on a day like this
I have seen
your faint smile.

So much depends on it, you say.
So strong are the lines anchored in the heart,
they lift the corners of the mouth,
the edges of the eyes,
they smooth the surface of the brow.

On a day like this, you say, only a faint smile will do.
You say, practice faithfully the half-smile while knowing
what you have seen you will see again.
Practice gently, moment to moment,
so the lines remain attached and elastic.

Practice until you can feel
the lines quiver
the corners move
and your heart lift
with your full smile.

TOGETHER IN HOPE

We sit anxiously knowing
the time has come.

Nervous fingers chisel doubt
across our brows.

Impatience draws fear
on tight lips.

Our hearts beat out the anger
in our chests.

Who will quiet our fingers,
relax our lips,
stop the pounding?

Who will rise to speak?
Who will sit to listen?
Will we do this
until we can move
together in hope?

FINDING SPACE

All the space I need to breathe freely has vanished. Even the
people I love best are too close for comfort. Fear fills the
space between me and others until only distance remains,
the distance between oil and flame. I push back, afraid this
black hole will fill me with nothingness.

Yet my breath rises, without thoughts, without fear. Like
the gift of the sun at dawn, a blessing lifts my soul into an
expanding universe, sacred space to reach out, to touch you
with loving kindness.

In Troubled Times

From the loneliness of troubled times, we come

To discover that we are not alone.

Into the dwelling place of togetherness, we come

To collect remnants of hope.

From fear that all is lost, we come

To discover what will save us.

Into the comfort of each other's arms, we come

To feel the strength that has not yet vanished.

From darkness, we come

To wait until our eyes begin to see.

Into the refuge of fading dreams, we come

To remove illusions and focus new visions.

From despair that walks alone, we come

To travel together.

Into the dwelling place of generations, we come

*To pledge allegiance to being peace
and doing justice.*

Keeping Spirits Up

Growing up Doan Viet Hoat learned the disciplines of Zen meditation and yoga from Buddhist monks and from his family. These gifts sustained him as he came of age in a sea of war, violence, and cruel oppression.

A series of events, however, would test the value of these gifts. Hoat had become a well-educated and influential man by the time the U.S.-supported South Vietnamese government began threatening and killing Buddhist monks that opposed their rule of terror. His activism and public protests eventually made him a government target and he was forced into exile. When he returned, the war was over and Communists were in power. They too feared the power of his voice and imprisoned him along with other intellectuals. He spent the next twelve years in a cell shared by forty other prisoners. Finally he was released, only to be detained again for two more years and then imprisoned in solitary confinement for another five and a half years.

Through all this Hoat said he wanted to send a message to the people that the dictators could not win by putting people in jail. That strong spirit of resistance was sustained through years of cruel imprisonment by his disciplined practice of yoga and Zen meditation. To keep his mind alert, he also wrote and recited poems that he had memorized. These practices kept his spirits up, preventing him from sinking into despair under his trying circumstances.

Teach Me Aliveness

Spirit of the vibrant life, something is numbing me and I am growing unaware of my own feelings. I fear it occupies my soul. I don't know when it first arrived, but it travels with me. Even the good works that I do seem routine and boring.

Blessed guide to my awakening, teach me what it means to be alive to each moment of my life. Grant me the wisdom to greet the moments of this day with exuberance. If sadness comes knocking, help me to unlock the door and welcome it with a warm embrace. Let me hold it until it falls asleep in my arms like a baby. If joy appears at my threshold, let me invite her in and dance freely with her until dawn, when a new guest will arrive. In the name of all that life has to offer, teach me the wisdom of being fully alive.

The Practiced Wait

Spirit of the practiced wait, guide me into the moments of my life when all that can be done has been done, and when all that ought to have been said has been said. When I arrive at these special moments, still my mind, my hands, my racing feet.

Then let me open wide my heart to feel all that flows through it—the painful and joyful memories, the shaped and unshaped hopes for the future. Hold back from my lips the cry, "How long must I wait?"

Help me accept the wisdom of the proverb: *All things come to those who wait.*

Tell the Good News

Jesus of Nazareth was one of the great storytellers. He knew that real-life experiences are the subtext of every good story. He was not thinking of the abstract ideal to "love thy neighbor" when he began the story of the Good Samaritan. Rather, he must have seen or heard of a similar situation that so moved him he wanted to shape what happened into a pithy good news parable.

It is easy to share bad news. Many may have heard of that ancient robbery and how good people walked past the wounded stranger. Yet, Jesus told the good news of the one man who stopped to help. We too can choose which stories to tell and which news to share. When we share good news we give form to our longing for peace and justice.

The Proof

I can lay no claim to goodness until I can prove that mean people have not made me mean.

—Barbara Kingsolver

Across the vast expanse of apathy,
deep in the dark space of mindlessness,
hidden in constellations of greed,
lost in black holes of anger,
the silence of the universe whispers to me:

> Be Passionate Awareness
> Be Selfless Compassion
> Be Peaceful Justice

Seek Passion

Passion lops off the bough of weariness.

—Rumi

The sounds of war, torture, and unspeakable cruelty pound in my ears. Day after day, year after year, they beat a numbing rhythm into my soul. The rapacious drone of evil can deafen symphonies of hope. Without rest, the soul goes into arrhythmia, followed by compassion fatigue, action paralysis, and sometimes even death. I am sure that unless I consciously, deliberately, and periodically turn them off they will deafen me and the sweet music of sympathy, empathy, and love will vanish.

Passion for life's blessings is the elixir that renews. It can be experienced in moments of disengagement. It is an act of deep faith to look up from the work and listen as the wind whistles in the leaves or the songbird sings to the morning. There is a lot at stake in observing the beauty of life. Passion grows with each fleeting observation.

Oh, don't sigh heavily from fatigue, Rumi says. Seek passion, seek passion, seek passion!

BALANCING

Grieving dreams that have passed away,

We wait for night vision.

Marching to unfinished music,

We listen for whispers of wisdom.

Seeing the cost of impatience,

We take slow steps for change.

Sensing the price of waiting,

We take steps with courage.

Letting go of innocence,

We touch our guilt with forgiveness.

Silencing prideful talk,

We lift up what has not been done.

Moving from solitude,

We walk side-by-side.

Balancing our dreams with reality,

We live in hope.

MISSED OPPORTUNITY

I was hungry and you gave me no food, I was thirsty and you gave me nothing to drink.

—Matthew 25:42

The board meeting of our inner-city church was going reasonably well. We had worked through half the agenda when a disheveled man entered the room through an unlocked door. One of the board members got up quickly and with a polite firmness told the man there was a private meeting going on and that the building was not open to the public at this time. Pausing only to hand the man a list of places he could go for help, the board member closed and locked the door, then took his seat. A potentially disruptive situation had been handled with appropriate kindness, or so it seemed.

The next day, I became increasingly unsettled by what had happened. The momentary discomfort of the street person's arrival had passed—and with it an opportunity to practice compassionate hospitality. Oh, there were reasons enough to justify handling the situation as we did. After all, we were running an institution that did good works in the community. The board member had not only politely dismissed the man, but had handed him a list of places we had carefully prepared.

But the scene still gnawed at my heart. For while we had practiced a small act of kindness, we failed to open our hearts to the stranger. Perhaps we could have interrupted our meeting for five minutes, given him a cup of coffee, and invited him to sit in the entrance way a while before sending him away. One of us could have sat and listened to him for a few moments. Perhaps we could have made sure he arrived safely at the place we sent him. The list of missed opportunities clicked off in my mind.

The problem that evening was not that the door was unlocked, but that our hearts remained closed. Institutions, even those dedicated to helping others, often separate and divide us from one another. They absolve us from practicing bold acts of hospitality that can save us from the numbing effects of radical disconnection. The spiritual practice most needed in our full-agenda lives is compassionately connecting with others where and when we meet them.

WAITING MOMENTS

Blessed guide in my waiting moment, help me listen to the songs in my soul. When all that could be done has been done, when all that ought to have been said has been spoken, come to me. Still my mind, my hands, and my mouth, that I might hear what is expected of me. If I should ask, "How long must I wait?" whisper to me that I have already arrived. Help me see that in this waiting moment the shaman has drawn out the sickness of impatience and satisfied my deepest longing to be of use. May I always bless the waiting moment of my life.

THE IMPERATIVE TO PRAISE

We have borrowed these
    clothes, these time-and-space personalities,
from a light, and when we praise, we pour
    them back in.

—Rumi

Is the glass half-empty or is it half-full? The usual answer is that it is a matter of perspective. The "half-empty" people emphasize scarcity, the "half-full" people opportunity. But life is more than perspective. What if the fullness of the glass depends not on how we view its contents, but on how much we pour back into it? Life is not a zero-sum game to be divided into halves, or quarters, or thirds, but a flowing river that receives our poured-out time-and-space personalities. If we fail to pour freely we will most surely become empty.

Finding Harmony

Spirit of gathering and belonging, draw me out of my loneliness and self-doubt. Pull me away from my fears of self-exposure into the comforting and challenging presence of others. Here in the sacred spaces between people and groups, play for me the notes that harmonize with those I have shaped in solitude. Here, where differences are made clear and kindred spirits discovered, help me compose the lasting meaning of my life. Remind me to practice patiently until I can confidently and compassionately play the music of justice and peace in the great halls of social engagement.

The Right Voice

Today they tell me I'm going to Chiapas, to lead the people on a march into the community of La Realidad. When we get to the roadblock, there will be armed paramilitaries . . . My fear disappears when I begin to speak in these situations, without raising my voice.

—Patria Jiménez

Patria Jiménez, the first openly homosexual member of the Mexican Congress, had good reason to fear when she led that march in Chiapas. In a two-year period, twenty-five transgender people had been systematically assassinated there.

Our voices can rise when we are afraid or they can become mute. The raised voice rages and the mute voice stifles. Jiménez chose neither. Instead, she spoke without raising her voice. She said that her ability to do this came from knowing that she was not alone and that each time she acts in the face of her fear the movement for equality advances a little. When, with courage, we take strong action with others, our fears can disappear and our voices can be heard more clearly.

BE WORTHY

To look for the future in the mirror of this moment

Is to be worthy of the name presence.

To count your blessings instead of your accomplishments

Is to be worthy of the name humble.

To accept without malice the judgment of others

Is to be worthy of the name kind.

To speak without anger when anger is justified

Is to be worthy of the name patience.

To give unselfishly when all has been lost

Is to be worthy of the name generous.

To be honest when deceit is expedient

Is to be worthy of the name truth-teller.

To act when realism demands pessimism

Is to be worthy of the name hope.

To move forward when the way is not clear

Is to be worthy of the name faith.

To abandon conformity when it compromises justice

Is to be worthy of the name courage.

To make your enemy's well-being your own concern

Is to be worthy of the name peacemaker.

To know that your humble, kind, and generous presence
brings faith, courage, and hope

Is to be worthy of the name wisdom.

SIDE BY SIDE

The rain had stopped and in a patchwork of puddles outside
the church, the purple setting sun mingled naturally with the
blue sky. The images of what I had seen in that church, and
in the small building next to it, were not, however, blending
so easily in my mind. The church was beautiful, but cement-
ed into the walls of the small building were row upon row of
the skulls of the church's enemies.

I had come to this part of what was then Yugoslavia to
study religion and economics. I knew of the religious hatreds
that had defined life there for centuries, but I was not prepared for this—the stark juxtaposition of that sacred building and the building of skulls.

My heart was opened that day by those contrasting symbols, side by side. While the grayness of twilight or dawn have
their place, so too do the symbols of noon and midnight.

Today when my vision is unfocused and I am lost in inde-
cisive grayness, I practice an act of symbolic clarity. I move
two objects on my desk closer together. One is a small piece
of shrapnel that landed near a friend of mine while he was at
war. The other is a small wooden chalice with a flame carved
into it—a symbol of my faith in the eternal presence of love.
I let those objects sit close to each other as they do naturally
in my heart when it is open. Then I ask myself what action I
must take to bring alive the symbol of life-giving goodness.
The sacred must always stand close to the profane as witness to the possibility of living in ways that affirm the best
in humanity.

CONNECTION ADDICTION

Newspapers, magazines, books, and stacks of *Congressional Records* surrounded me. The waves of radio and television newscasts crashed over me from morning to night. I had convinced myself that this was an essential part of doing my job as a broadcast journalist. In reality, I was an information addict and it was controlling my life.

My addiction took hold long before the disease of connectivity became epidemic. Today the pervasiveness of cell phones, iPods, and the Internet makes it hard for anyone to limit his or her daily intake of information.

One day friends asked my daughter and me to join them on a trip to an amusement park. I said I was too busy working on a documentary. In disgust my friends responded, "You know, there is more to life than the news." The truth must have hurt, because I went on the trip. That day, I heard no newscasts and read no newspapers. Other sounds filled my heart that day, the sounds of laughing children and smiling couples. I began to admit that my world was too full of news.

In twelve-step programs, whether for alcohol, drugs, or gambling, the first step toward recovery is to admit to yourself the power the addiction has over your life. It would be a while longer until I hit bottom and confessed my addiction to others, and still longer until I established a practice of regularly disconnecting from the flow of information.

Today, I no longer wake up to newscasts or go to bed with them. Instead, I use that time to sit in silence or reflection. This small spiritual practice allows me to unite with a whole new source of vital information.

Do Nothing

Practice doing nothing each day.
    Not the whole day
    but that part of it when your soul
    feels pinched and shoved
    and crammed into the end of your pen,
    pressed against a deadline
    or the cushion of your computer chair,
    or hanging on the request
    from someone who wants one more thing from you
    and you can't say no.

Practice doing nothing each day.
    Make it a religious thing that binds you to a truth
    that can only be experienced,
    like when you breathe out and it empties you
    of all that presses against your chest from the inside
    until it spills out of you
    in angry words or impatient deeds.

Practice doing nothing each day.
    Fill your day with moments of nothingness,
    little ones at first, then stretch them,
    pull them until the muscles of all your undoing ache,
    like that time you felt them collapse
    after a long run, a hard swim, a heavy lift—
    as you heaved the last time
    before you said, "Enough."

Practice doing nothing each day.
    Until all your doings yield to a new habit
    that demands you do nothing
    and do it consciously, with your eyes wide open,
    mindfully, without attachment,
    skillfully, with balanced acts of waiting,
    before you return to the world of all your doing.

THINKING OF YOU WHEN YOU'RE DEAD

I think of you when you're dead.

The way the red reflection
of your energy will have faded
from your cheeks—those cheeks I kissed
after you blushed.

I think of you when you're dead
and all the dead others I have seen
run through me like a cold river
and I kiss them too.

My uncle and his mother's
inconsolable grief as she threw
herself on him in his casket.

My father and his anguished words as he reached for the
the glass that fell from his grasp
as he tried to take a last sip
before dying.

My childhood friend
whose war finally killed him
long after the battle was over
when he, with blood-stained hands, tried to heal others
who could not be saved.

I think of you when you're dead
and then I think about others
whose names I will never know
whose deaths moved me.

Those who evaporated in an instant
leaving shadows on a bridge in Hiroshima, or was it Nagasaki?
whose images, released on the twenty-fifth year of their dying,
shook my soul into perpetual war resistance.

The images of children burning
in piles outside of Auschwitz, or was it Dachau?
whose vapors fill the lungs
of other children in places like Bosnia, Rwanda,
Guatemala, Indonesia, Pakistan, Afghanistan, Iraq, Sudan,
on and on.

When I think of you when you're dead
I come alive
and want to kiss you
all the days of my life

and I want to kiss them
want to never stop kissing
all who are alive.

CAN YOU GRIEVE?

*I am deeply grieved, even to death; remain here, and stay awake
with me.*
                                        —Matthew 26:38

How could he help but grieve?
All was lost—and his ministry had failed.

He had dreamed
that people would cross the Jericho road with him
to help the hated Samaritans
but they did not follow him out
from their comfortable indifference.

He had dreamed
that people would turn their cheeks to shame the violent
but instead they reached for the sword
to defend him in his final hour.

He had dreamed
that people would give others the shirts off their backs
yet they let him, their best friend, die naked on a cross.

He had dreamed
that people would grow a mustard seed of their love
into a kingdom of kindness
but there was no kindness in their betrayal of him.

Have you dreamed enough to grieve as he did?

Have you grieved yet
for all you have lost by staying on the safe side of the road?
Have you grieved yet
for having reached for the sword or the sharp-edged word?
Have you grieved yet
for having not loved enough to practice kindness?

Can you grieve now with a wrenching cry
that will leave you limp, empty, exhausted,
cleansed of all that you have failed to do?
Can you grieve now so you can start anew
and dream what he dreamed?

BE COLLECTORS OF GOODNESS

Spirit of my ancient past, I have seen drawings on cave walls, in catacombs under cities, on mountain cliffs and desert canyons. I have watched the hand's touch refine and the cutting edge sharpen over time until the figures are full and the dimensions are deep. These drawings cannot be contained in museums, and weren't meant to be. They were created out of life, for life, to tell the story of life, that people might not perish.

Today let me paint a blooming tree and an open field on the wall of my heart. Strengthen my hand so I might etch images of children playing, of fledgling birds taking flight, of new-born animals standing ready to step out in the world. Teach me to gather all those things that tell the story of life's goodness, for certainly the ages have not been kind to goodness.

WHAT TO CALL YOU?

Spirit of life, I don't know what to call you. Sometimes, when I speak the names others have given you, my mouth feels full of marbles and I cannot form a distinct syllable. At other times, especially when I connive with others to make justice compassionately, I feel you are standing in front of me—a choir director—harmonizing the longings of my heart with others.

Perhaps I should call you silence and watch you rise like the mist of the morning before any word is spoken. At times I have given up calling you anything. But then, to whom would I express my thanks for being alive and for feeling the love of others? Or for the honor of spreading love in the world?

Even though I cannot express your name I need to address you. I need to feel that you are as close to me as my next breath. And I need to say thank you. So I think I will call you You and mean everything I can see, feel, touch, smell, and know. And I will know that You are more than all this and there is no need to speak except through acts of love, justice, and kindness.

ACCEPTING GRACE

Listen, o drop, give yourself up without regret,
and in exchange gain the Ocean.

Listen, o drop, bestow upon yourself this honor
and in the arms of the Sea be secure.

Who indeed would be so fortunate?
An ocean wooing a drop?

—Rumi

SURPRISE GIFTS

On the dirt floor of a Nazi concentration camp, prisoners sat listening to the rain after a meager meal. Among them was psychologist Viktor Frankl, who described the scene. After the rain stopped, a prisoner burst into the hovel and pleaded with his weary comrades to come outside. Reluctantly some picked themselves up and followed. Pointing up, where the setting sun hung in the Western sky, the prisoner said simply "Look."

In the midst of grief, tired to the bone, we are called to lift our heads and accept grace. Grace is a gift that comes unexpectedly. The sigh of relief, ripples of laughter, the quiet joys that lift heavy hearts, these are among its expressions. Discipline and practice can make us more aware of it, but they don't create it. Grace can be prayed for and hoped for, but it always arrives as a surprise. Whatever our beliefs, grace is one of those true wonders of being human that, if accepted, can change our view of the world.

TRUSTING UNCERTAINTY

Spirit of Life, God of Love, I have learned to trust the rhythm of your changing seasons. I delight in the certainty that each change, no matter how wrenching, brings with it the promise of new life. Yet in the affairs of my own days there are times when I lose my trust in the rhythms of change. In those moments, I pray to be reminded of how the dawn follows night and spring arrives only after winter has lost its grip on reality. Here, in the uncertainty of the moment, help me accept change with the delight of a child coming of age or an elder embracing new-found wisdom. When I long for the comforts of what can no longer be, lift my head above my losses and my fears and cast my eyes on the promise of new beginnings.

CONVERGENCE

Spirit of Life, God of history and god of nature, you seem to merge and flow in me, granting me the power to be planted here and the energy to grow with hope. History, for all its pain and trials, has bestowed upon me the opportunity to live my life doing justice and practicing peace. I pray that I will never turn these words into abstractions, but always see them as places to take my next steps for change. When the burden of my history and the unfolding story of the world wears me down, paralyzing my mind with hopelessness, help me feel the pulsing flow of life. When I look at my face and the contours of my body, no matter the challenges they present, help me see how I have been blessed awake to the dawn of a new day. Let me pause and give thanks for the energy, even if faint, that carries me into awareness.

A HOLY MOMENT

A white South African soldier was testifying before the Truth and Reconciliation Commission. Referring to a massacre of twenty members of the African National Congress, the soldier said, "We gave the orders to open fire." The room grew quiet. A long moment passed. And then another. Then the soldier spoke again, "Please forgive us." Silence followed, then applause. Sensing the spirit of forgiveness, Archbishop Desmond Tutu said, "We are in the presence of something holy."

Something holy enters our lives when we speak the painful truth of what we have done as individuals or groups. Without speaking such truth, forgiveness will never be offered to us.

Finding Thanksgiving

Spirit of Life, God of Love, let me write a thanksgiving on my heart. In clean lines I will inscribe what pleases me: a warm autumn day, a quickly spreading smile on a child's face, the still-warm touch of an aging loved one. Then I will write the names of all who have been with me at moments of great discernment. Let gratitude pour from my soul as I recall their gifts of time, patience, and unconditional love. I will draw empty lines for those whom I will never know, who gave needed gifts to my mentors.

In this world of endless distractions and complications, I pray for the wisdom to humble myself in gratitude for these gifts beyond measure. Help me learn to thankfully give them to others.

Hold the Holy

When we can no longer grasp
what holds us upright,

When we wring our hands in grief
for the living,

Only then can we tunnel with clenched fingers
into the depths of a peace that passes understanding,
where we will find our losses, our uncertainties,
and all our denials.

Struggling with clubbed hands, we will turn locks
rusted by tears of regret and neglect.

Only then will the treasured vessel inside
break and pour its healing ointment
onto our hands, slowly opening them
to hold,
then lift,
the holy to the troubled surface of life.

Eternal Light

If you spend yourselves in behalf of the hungry and satisfy the needs of the oppressed, then your light will rise in the darkness, and your night will become like the noonday.

—Isaiah 58:10

The struggle to feed the hungry and free the oppressed is daunting. The heart is quickly overwhelmed by the magnitude of the task. To find light in the darkest of circumstances, with the odds against you, is not easy. But the Hebrew prophet Isaiah asserts that justice work itself carries with it a built-in light switch that will make our night *like the noonday*.

I was sitting in a court room the first time I saw a person with a glowing internal light. He faced the judge with a confident, pleasant countenance. He explained why he refused to pay his taxes. "I have no objection to paying my taxes," he said, "but my conscience will not allow me to contribute to our government's war effort. That money should be spent to feed the hungry." At that moment you could see the light of noonday spread across the room.

The reward for spending ourselves for a just cause is discovering the eternal light within us and knowing that it will turn on as we work for peace and justice.

Born in Darkness

Our bodies were formed in a darkness that light could not penetrate. There all the mystery and power of the universe gathered to be awakened at the moment of birth.

Today we live in another darkness. Feeling powerless to push out, we find little promise in our circumstance. Engulfed by inadequacies, we reach for the grim tools of revenge and cynicism.

Spirit of ever-renewing cycles, grant us patience to forge new instruments of peace. Grant us the wisdom to know that life will again gather the vital energy needed for our rebirth.

The Heart Lives in Darkness

When we see long dark days ahead, it is hard to be thankful. What little light there was fades and our vision of hope vanishes.

We pray now, not for victory, and certainly not for yesterday's plans. Today our prayer moves inward, where our most vital organ lives in darkness. Contracting and expanding, our hearts remind us that life-sustaining work is sometimes done best in dark, out-of-sight places.

Who Is Speaking?

It is not I who speak, but the wind.
Wind blows through me.
Long after me is the wind.
　　　　　　　　　　—Marge Piercy

Leaving the pulpit after the first time it happened, I felt emptied of all anxiety and vanity. What happened? I asked myself. Who was that speaking? The second time it happened, someone spoke of seeing an aura above me. I smiled, and then quickly turned my mind to practical concerns. Since then there have been other times. All of them leaving me wondering where my words came from, and why they moved others. Each time my ego claimed ownership, or I said that I was "giving voice" to a particular cause or concern, the mystery disappeared.

Martin Luther King Jr. wanted to impress the congregation of the Dexter Avenue Baptist Church in Montgomery Alabama, so that they would call him to be their minister. He wondered whether he should try to impress them with his scholarship or focus on an inspirational theme. He decided on the latter and told himself: "Keep Martin Luther King Jr. in the background and God in the foreground and everything will be all right." Sometimes that is all it takes to feel the wind blow through you.

How Do You Suffer?

How do you suffer?
In silence,
with raging anger,
with pestering complaints?

When do you suffer?
As the sun rises,
as it sets?

What do you suffer?
The sharp edge of violence,
the blunt force of indifference,
the loss of truth, youth, or love?

With whom do you suffer?
With him, with her, with us
or alone?

Ask these questions a thousand times
and before you speak
the silence
will draw from your suffering
the compassion of Buddha,
the passion of Christ,
the wisdom of Muhammad.

Ask these questions a thousand times
and become the peace you seek,
the justice you long for.

I Am Wonderfully Made

Spirit of Life, God of Love, too often I run from you. Breathless with fear, I seek refuge in judgmental words against others or in places filled with self-righteous anger.

Let the words of your psalmist penetrate my hiding places. "I am wonderfully made." Great Spirit of Hope, grant me the wisdom to accept this simple truth and know that whatever my weaknesses and imperfections, I cannot hide from your loving spirit or flee the healing power of your presence.

Look and Listen

Look for peace here
    on maps marked by other travelers
        in their foldings and unfoldings of desire.

Look for peace here
    in the moving circles of stars
        in their beckoning gestures of hope.

Look for peace here
    on the labyrinth shelves of libraries
        in their stacks of wisdom and reason.

Look for peace here
    in the shifting layers of ages
        in their unmarked deposits of glory and defeat.

Listen for peace here
    in the everyday melodies of love
        in their brief rests and pauses.

Listen for peace here
    in the rhythm of work and leisure
        in its boredom and excitement.

Listen for peace here
    on the crests of waves crashing and pounding
        in their deep currents of debris settling.

Listen for peace here
    on the winds roaring and whispering
        in the surface-water rippling.

Look and Listen

For what is essential for peace has arrived
    bringing you
        all you need to see,
           all you need to hear,
               all you need to find
                  to make peace.

IN A WHIRLWIND

Spirit of Life, God of Love, at times we are caught in a whirl-wind. Its force overwhelms us, threatening to lift us off the ground of our very being. As it churns up all that we thought was well rooted, we begin to whirl frantically in meaning-less motion. Then clinging and grasping for some certainty to hold onto, we grow weary with despair. Frightened, we watch as everything familiar is blown away and our dearest hopes vanish. When will the destruction stop? When will the winds calm? The answers escape us.

    Spirit of our longing hearts, grant us the wisdom to find that quiet center within us. When the storms rage, lead us inward to find the peace that passes all understanding. And when we find that place of quiet strength, let us be of comfort to others who are also caught in the whirlwinds of their lives.

Seeing in Darkness

In a dark time the eye begins to see.
          —Theodore Roethke

Spirit of the coming darkness, forgive me for not welcoming your return. I have learned to fear you, remembering how once you pushed joy out of my soul, and how once you blinded me as I traveled a winding road. The truth is, I don't trust or understand you, and I quickly curse you.

Yet, in today's twilight I sense a strange comfort in your approach. With courage, I resist lighting my candle. A soothing night song accompanies you. I hear it singing, "Don't run, don't leave. I have a gift for you." I wait a long time, and then, just past midnight, when your darkness seems complete, I hear you sing again, "Don't run, don't leave. I have a gift for you."

Now with my eyes open wide in darkness, I begin to see the gifts of your spirit.

A Strange Gift

It's hard to explain. It's perhaps a kind of gift that you have inside yourself.
          —Abubacar Sultan

Abubacar Sultan couldn't study, go to classes, or teach. The images of the children haunted him until he had to do something to save as many as he could. In his war-torn homeland of Mozambique, 250,000 children were displaced and another 200,000 were orphaned between 1985 and 1992. Sultan put himself in the midst of that war to find and identify children and bring them to safety. Many of the children had witnessed or been forced to commit acts of violence and murder, sometimes against members of their own families. He trained five hundred people in therapies to help traumatized children. Sultan's efforts helped save 20,000 children during that war. When it was over, he continued to work to help by registering children's births. His work, begun when he was 24 years old, won him international recognition and spread the lessons of his projects to other countries.

A practicing Muslim, Sultan thinks that the reason he risked his life for the children of Mozambique "lies partly in religion and partly in education." Yet, he adds, "It must be something deeper, something inside."

It is a strange gift that Sultan was given, this inner need to act. These kinds of impulses rest uncomfortably inside us and can emerge unpredictably to change everything we expect to do. When these gifts make themselves known they often demand of us what reason will not dare and prudence will not risk.

JOY IN DARK TIMES

The spiritual call to acknowledge blessings in the midst of suffering transcends time and theology. It proclaims that joy is not the absence of pain and suffering, but the affirmation that life is always worthy of our reverent attention.

The ancient Hebrew psalmist implored all creatures to *make a joyful noise unto God.* He didn't say to make a joyful noise only when we are happy. After asserting the first Noble Truth that life is suffering, the Buddha became the smiling and laughing enlightened one. In the Christian book of Galatians we read: *But the fruit of the Spirit is love, joy, peace [and] longsuffering.* Through a paradox of faith, human suffering is linked with the spirit of God. The Hindu Noble Laureate Rabindranath Tagore put it yet another way: *All the . . . evils in the world have overflowed their banks, yet oarsmen, take your places with the blessing of sorrow in your souls.*

It is impossible to intellectually understand the paradox that eternally links joy and suffering. But every day we are offered the blessing to experience it.

The Mystic's Gift

Come in,
you masters of the universe,
you creators of new worlds,
who would remake in your image all I have given.

Come in,
you great doers of good deeds,
you givers of blessed mercies,
who have comforted the wounded and the sick.

Come in,
you who hunger and thirst after righteousness,
I will give you rest.

Leave outside my temple
your heartfelt longings,
your wisdom of the ages,
the blueprints for your "city on a hill."

Leave before my threshold
all you have created for my glory
and done for my pleasure.

Leave your sacred books
your rings of certainty
and crosiers of power.

Come in and I will give you rest
in the sanctuary of the eternal now
where I will make you in my image, again,
and bestow on you
the meaning of love everlasting.

Doing It Matters

God of Love, Spirit of my greatest longing, grant me the courage to look out, with open eyes, upon this broken and bleeding world. Let me not blink nor turn away, but focus on that one important thing I can do today to affirm the worth and dignity of another. Grant me the wisdom to start with those close at hand who need my understanding, patience, and words of encouragement. Then lift my face, that I might see those in the distance, whose circumstances have bent them low, or whose captors have held them down too long. When I have looked a long time at such cruelty and my mind grows weary with thoughts of my own impotence, challenge me to not plead my weakness. Silence me before I speak such blasphemy. Break through my self-absorption that I might accept what I am capable of doing and know that doing it matters.

Re-Creation

Spirit of Life, God of Love, who are we to know how you moved over the waters when all was new? We were not there when you parted them and formed dry land. We didn't hear you cry with joy when earth gave birth to life, or when love began to grow in the human heart. Your longing for hope created this vast diversity of beings with whom we now share our days.

Spirit of perpetual creation and re-creation, help us to see past our pride to what we have done. Help us accept responsibility for destroying the gifts of clean water and air, of woodlands and grasslands, of creatures that fly through the air and swim through the seas and walk, creep, and crawl on dry land. Help us to gather the seeds of humility and join you in renewing the earth.

Come to Me

Come to me when my soul can't feel another's pain,

> *We will awaken your impulse to heal.*

Come to me when my soul trembles in fear,

> *We will awaken your courage to love.*

Come to me when my soul rages with anger,

> *We will awaken your longing for peace.*

Come to me when my soul whines,

> *We will awaken your power to see beyond yourself.*

Come to me when my soul dries with bitterness,

> *We will awaken your tears of regret and instill new hope.*

Come to me when my soul feels empty,

> *We will awaken you and you will know you are not alone.*

An Inkling

Spirit of my mind and senses, pray with me now, that I might accept the limits of my knowledge and perceptions. Open me to what is hidden and can only be expressed in symbols, never spoken—not even with words that have echoed in sacred places, shaped by generations of good people. Grant me an inkling of your presence when my heart is stirred to rejoice and I give thanks for being alive.

KNOWLEDGE

The Spirit knows what we have seen—
hungry lives, broken dreams
bodies flung on soldiers' fields
a righteous pose that never yields

The Spirit knows what we have heard
growls of hate, biting words
cries of pain from a lonely child
mournful notes of a chapel choir

The Spirit knows the forceful touch
a desperate grab, a seizing clutch
fists of anger, the fighter's jab
the coldness of a mortician's slab

But the Spirit knows much more than this
she knows the love in a child's kiss
she's watched love travel through unseen gates
and spied those moments it dispelled hate

The Spirit knows what we have seen
and moves us toward
a newer dream

BLESSED HALF-LIGHT

I paused to watch the yellow twilight spread across the living room. This gentle warning of the approaching darkness transformed the moment into a timeless and comforting event. The unexpected arrival of an old friend could not have changed my mood more quickly. With a comforting certainty, the half-light settled on sun-faded furniture, softening all in preparation for the night. The white walls turned cream and the amber shade on a treasured family floor lamp reflected light even though it was not on.

I too let go of my sharp edges and glowed softly, effortlessly. No rush of urgency pulsed through my veins, no unfinished task crossed my mind. As the yellow light shifted with the advent of darkness, I too felt changed.

Sometimes darkness enters the rooms of our hearts in this way, preparing us for what is to come.

EVOCATIVE EVIDENCE

I couldn't help staring at the result of my neighbor's hard day's labor. He had cut down a tree at the edge of his property and dug out its roots. When it was alive I hardly noticed it, but now it captured my imagination. With roots pointing up and trunk pointing down it looked like a homeless creature from the underworld. My stare revealed my heart's longing to get to know this creature. Before I could speak, my neighbor told me I could have it. Together we strained to get it into my wheel-barrel, and I deposited my new treasure in a neglected corner of my garden.

In the spring the melting snow exposed the tree and it spoke to me. It called me into its presence and began questioning me: "Who guards your roots? Who will give them strength to hold you firm when the winds of change and uncertainty blow? Who will give them resilience? Or stand quietly waiting until your imagination needs awakening?" "I never thought of that," I replied. In that moment I realized that my relationship with this fellow creature gave me powers that I needed.

I rolled my new friend to an honored place overlooking my garden and thought how good it was to know that someone was watching over the very ground of my being.

WHAT'S TO LEARN

Humanity has simply not yet learned to be happy and count its blessings.

—Robert Muller

What's to learn,

Everyone counts on someone.

What's to learn,

Life pulses, gushes, cries out with joy.

What's to learn,

Laughter liberates the soul from fear.

What's to learn,

The tender touch heals.

What's to learn,

Liberty yearns, grows, then pushes aside cowardice
and breathes in freedom.

What's to learn,

Grief, loss, and tragedy arrive
depart and return.

What's to learn,

Laughter, joy, and fulfillment
come and go.

What's to learn,

Happiness is knowing you are part of all this
and that you count.

CONSIDERATIONS

Consider the stars, their numbers
and the vastness of the cosmos.
Consider the mountains, how they rise above the tree line,
then slowly slide into the sea.
Consider the dust of ages, how it covers
traces of civilizations that gathered as we do.
Consider the empires, how they rose and fell
where deserts now blow and jungles now creep.
Consider the billions who staked their lives on love
and lost, never knowing what came next.

Considering all this, my small heart grows numb.
Considering all this, what does it matter what I do?
Then you touch me and I feel the universe awaken
and I know I am truly blessed.

SUPPOSE

Suppose you scrub your ethical skin until it shines,
but inside there is no music,
then what?

—Kabir

Suppose you cried a thousand tears for a child who died
when she drank bad water.

Suppose you organized a great movement
to clean the water.

Suppose you carried the first filled glass
to the child's sister.

Suppose you lifted it to her lips.

Suppose you watched her dive into the glass,
splash, and swim on.

OUR COMMON PURPOSE

This moment is beautiful,

For we have gathered.

This moment is beautiful,

*For we have gathered
in common purpose.*

This moment is beautiful,

*For we have gathered
in common purpose
to do important work.*

This moment is beautiful,

*For we have gathered
in common purpose
to do important work
that only we can do.*

This moment is beautiful,

*For together
we recreate the world.*

FOR FURTHER READING

Dyer, Adam Lawrence. *Love Beyond God: Meditations.* Boston: Skinner House, 2016.

Gilbert, Richard. *The Prophetic Imperative: Social Gospel in Theory and Practice,* Second Edition. Boston: Skinner House, 2001.

Morrison-Reed, Mark, and Jacqui James, eds. *Been in the Storm So Long.* Boston: Skinner House, 1991.

————. *Voices from the Margins: An Anthology of Meditations.* Boston: Skinner House, 2012.

Nelson, Brian. *Earth Bound: Daily Meditations for All Seasons.* Boston: Skinner House, 2004.

Parker, Rebecca. *Blessing the World: What Can Save Us Now.* Boston: Skinner House, 2006.

Rothberg, Donald. *The Engaged Spiritual Life: A Buddhist Approach to Transforming Ourselves and the World.* Boston: Beacon Press, 2006.

Safford, Victoria, ed. *With or Without Candlelight: A Meditation Anthology.* Boston: Skinner House, 2009.

Schulz, F. William. *In Our Own Best Interest: How Defending Human Rights Benefits All.* Boston: Beacon Press, 2002.

Sinkford, William G., ed. *To Wake, To Rise: Meditations on Justice and Resilience.* Boston: Skinner House, 2017.